THE POCKET MANAGER

By the same author

SUPERMAN
THE NAKED MANAGER
CAN YOU TRUST YOUR BANK? (with Norris Williatt)
THE COMMON MILLIONAIRE
THE EUROPEAN REVENGE (with Norris Williatt)
THE NAKED INVESTOR
THE ONCE AND FUTURE MANAGER
THE BUSINESS OF WINNING
THE BUSINESS OF SUCCESS
THE NAKED MARKET
THE SUPERMANAGERS (revised version of *The Business of Success*)
THE NEW NAKED MANAGER

THE POCKET MANAGER

Robert Heller

Hodder & Stoughton

LONDON SYDNEY AUCKLAND TORONTO

British Library Cataloguing in Publication Data

Heller, Robert, *1932–*
    The pocket manager.
    1. Management
    I. Title
    658   HD31

ISBN 0-340-38818-8

To Angela

A

ABC ANALYSIS – Ranking inventory by three classes (ABC) of descending "usage value" – that is, class A will consist of the 20% of the inventory items which, as Pareto's Law will tell you, account for 80% of the movements in and out of the inventory. Obviously, you concentrate attention on the class A goods in the warehouse and don't waste too much time on the less significant Cs. (*See also*: Pareto's Law.)

ABOVE-THE-LINE – Two unrelated meanings here, both the opposite of below-the-line. Both above and below have different senses, one financial, the other marketing. Financially, above the line is where they keep the profits – so a firm that charges R&D as a current expenditure (which it should) puts it *above* the line.

A foolish firm, though, would treat R&D as a capital item and set it below that line – thus inflating the profits *above*. Neither accounting approach, of course, makes a penny's worth of difference to the underlying value of the company. Below the line, though, is a perfectly legitimate place to stow away exceptional items that really shouldn't be charged against current income.

In marketing, above-the-line expenditure is obviously a current expense – it's advertising: in the press, on TV, radio, or anywhere else. Below-the-line spending is plainly just as current, but refers to promotional spending: free gifts, sponsorship, in-store displays, competitions.

8 Absorption

ABSORPTION – What you absorb are overheads, or fixed costs. How you absorb them is by attributing a proportion of costs to whatever it is you're producing. These are the indirect costs that can't be allocated to any one part of the operation: any competent management accountant can work out suitable percentages that can be applied as an addition to the direct costs which you do know.

The system stands in contrast to marginal costing. Here you don't try to allocate costs to particular products. Instead, you recover them from the margin between revenue and direct costs. The point where recovery is complete is the break-even point – when all the costs have been duly absorbed, and every subsequent sale makes a profit.

ACID TEST – If a business can't pass the acid test, it can't do anything else – because it's on the way to bankruptcy. You count up the current assets (that is, cash or assets convertible to cash), and you also add up the current liabilities (the bills that have to be paid more or less forthwith).

Comparing the two gives the liquidity ratio (which equals the money owed to the firm, plus bank cash, plus cash in hand, divided by the current liabilities). Unless the answer is at least one (that is, the assets equal the liabilities), the business can't pay its bills and it's on the threshold of insolvency.

ACQUISITION – Growth by acquisition is the opposite of organic growth, but not its contradiction. That is, the object of an acquiring company will normally include making the acquisition grow by internal means. Indeed, unless it does, the purchase is most unlikely to prove justified financially – since good acquisitions usually come at a good price (or a bad one, depending on which way you look at it).

Acquiring companies fall into two broad categories: those whose business is acquisition (like Hanson Trust and other conglomerates), and those that acquire from time to time, for real or imaginary strategic reasons – for example, making horizontal or vertical mergers, or moving into entirely new fields either in search of faster-growing markets or to spread the company's risks more widely, or both.

Whatever the style and purpose of the acquiring company, the common feature of all acquisitions is that they carry a price. How high that price goes, and what form the price is paid in, have a profound and fundamental bearing on the acquiring company's own finances. Overpaying in relation to the profits generated by the acquisition will drag down the overall return on capital: buying a company for equity on a higher price-earnings multiple than your own will dilute your own earnings per share; financing a big deal by way of debt could push the debt-equity ratio dangerously high.

Despite all these well-known difficulties, and the others, equally well-known, of blending in the management of the acquired firm, the hunt for acquisitions is never-ceasing, and the demand for the services of investment bankers and other corporate marriage brokers is insatiable. They profit from the fact that acquiring a ready-made business is faster and easier, for all the hazards, than building one from scratch. (*See also*: Horizontal Integration; Vertical Integration; Debt-Equity Ratio.)

ACTION LEARNING – Should be one of the best-known types of management education instead of the least. The reason for its neglect is that it doesn't take place in business schools – or in any kind of school. The student manager learns by tackling an actual problem in a real company – preferably not his own.

The only academic help provided is coaching and monitoring during the action-learning assignment, plus topping up with any specific knowledge the manager needs for that job. But it's not only the academics who object to this obviously great idea. Managers are generally none too excited about having strangers wandering around the premises solving their problems – even if the host managers can, as a *quid pro quo*, send one of their own people elsewhere to enjoy the same excellent education.

It truly is excellent. One major, similar scheme for turning engineers into top production executives has achieved almost

100% success, both in solving the problems and getting people into good jobs. That's exactly what the prophet of Action Learning, Professor Reg Revans, would have predicted. Whatever the academics think, you can expect the action-learning principle – that of learning by project-based experience – to gain ground as the business school philosophy, learning by instruction, probably recedes somewhat: perhaps more than somewhat.

ADDED VALUE – A shiny new concept which is actually as old as the hills. The value added is simply the difference between (a) the cost of all materials and services bought in from outside the firm and (b) the revenue earned from outsiders by the goods and services sold. Why has this simple formula received any attention? What can it add to the familiar notions of profit, contribution, and loss?

One answer is that profit is a residual: what's left after everything else (except dividends) has been deducted. What it's deducted from, though, is nothing less than added value. That simple difference between (a) and (b) is the pool from which shareholders draw their dividends, lenders their interest – and workers their wages. It also finances the firm's investment in the future, without which it won't have one. It thus follows that if the value added is too low, or if anybody going to the well takes out too much water, somebody or something is going to suffer.

So a ratio to added value (like that of labour costs) can tell much about the health of the firm. It's also an excellent way of presenting that health to interested parties: particularly to workers, to demonstrate that no more money can be paid out in wages – unless they can help raise AV (by cutting costs or increasing yields). This idea has become the basis of some often elaborate schemes for linking pay to performance. It's a more effective method than profit sharing, because the AV formula is simpler to understand and has the virtue of drawing attention to the exact place (widening the gap between costs and prices) where the worker can make his contribution felt.

But the reason why the Japanese use the phrase "added value" so much is different again. They aim for products where they can "add the greatest value" – meaning those which, because of their market appeal and technological content, achieve the highest mark-up over the bought-in costs. They shun like the plague products where, because of the market situation or the production process, little or no value can be added. The analysis is fundamentally important, not just to profitability (however you calculate it), but to the strength of the company's stance in the marketplace. Value is added by brains rather than brawn – and the brainiest companies never take their eyes off that simple, vital AV statistic.

AI – Artificial Intelligence is looming larger and larger – or nearer and nearer. The computer so far has been dumb – its cleverness has stemmed only from slavishly obeying human commands in a way that the human, non-electronic brain can't match. But computers are coming closer to being able to reason, learn, solve problems, develop their own abilities.

The better the computer becomes in these respects, the more valuable it will become as an aide (rather than an aid) to management. Already (as in chess) the computer can solve problems. It can also test propositions by searching a database for evidence to support or refute them. Then there's the expert system, which acts as a consultant for the manager.

AI is the objective, the Holy Grail, of the pursuit of a fifth-generation computer, which has sparked a no-holds-barred race between the United States and Japan. The outcome of this electronic warfare could include computers that can translate from any language into any language (including computer language) and which, being able to recognise shapes, could enormously increase the flexibility of robots – and their intelligence. (*See also*: Expert Systems.)

AIDA – Nothing to do with Verdi. It is an acronym that stands for "Attention, Interest, Desire, Action", – these being the four stages through which the smart salesman should lead a prospect in sequence: first catching his Attention, then arousing his Interest, converting interest into Desire for the product, and then getting him to Act – preferably by signing a contract on the dotted line.

AIDED RECALL – The contrasting method to unaided recall. The researcher trying to discover if an advertisement has been effective recalls it to the interviewees – usually by showing it – and asks them if they remember the ad. Not regarded as so telling a method as the unaided variety; but neither way tells so much as direct response about whether the advertising money has done more than finance lunches at Langans. (*See also*: Unaided Recall; Direct Response.)

ALLOCATION PROBLEM – The management science terminology for what is actually the constant concern of management – how to achieve the best possible end-result from the use of available resources, given the fact that they are limited and that the alternative uses compete with each other in demands on those resources.

The expert attempting to solve this "programming problem" aims at optimisation: just like the manager he is advising. Assignment problems are a sub-genus of such difficulties: in these, you can only use one unit of a resource for each alternative purpose – so you're bound to have equal numbers of uses and resources.

On what's usually quite a narrow front, the allocation problem rubs in the basic broad truth that even an IBM can't do everything. Management must do the best it can with the best information and tools at its command. (*See also*: Optimisation.)

AMORTISATION – In its pure meaning, setting aside a sum annually to pay off a loan. In its currently applied sense, it means counting a part of the profits from a fixed asset against the cost. When the costs have been covered, the piece of machinery or whatever is said to be "fully amortised".

The word, while it is still used for the depreciation of intangible assets (like the cost of patents), isn't of much use in the modern factory. There, far more important considerations – like cost and ease of manufacture – determine when you replace plant, amortised or not.

APPRAISAL – You can't manage people without appraising them: that is, making a judgment on their personality and performance. You *can* manage people without telling them what you think on either subject. But that's not a good idea in the first place, because people respond, usually positively, to both praise and blame; and in the second place, big companies in particular are unlikely to let you get away without appraising as a boss and being appraised as a subordinate.

The more meticulous the company is generally, the more elaborate and important its appraisal system is likely to be. In a company like IBM, appraisal plays a crucial role in the corporate culture and in individual progress. But it's not easy to make formal appraisal work well – partly because managers often shy away from what one writer calls "frank, objective feedback". They pull their punches, and the subordinate, who's no keener than anybody else to be criticised, goes along.

This kind of difficulty explains why many systems force the manager to put a hard rating on his appraisal, assessing the subordinate on a scale from "excellent" to "poor or inadequate". Personnel departments love this approach because they can tie it in not only with salary reviews but also with planning management development. (The computer loves it, too.) But neither use exploits appraisal as it's supposed to be used – to produce better performance from the appraised and a better understanding of why he's performing well or badly from the appraiser.

The formal appraisal review can't do either on its own: it can only help as part of a continuing process of coaching, encouragement, interaction and criticism (preferably constructive). If the manager has to be reminded about these duties by a formal interview requirement, it won't help. If he doesn't need reminding, he doesn't need the interview, either. In such a case appraiser and appraised are both best advised to be cynical and play the system for what it's worth: the subordinate to get the highest possible rating put down on paper, the boss to use the interview to strengthen his own objectives vis-à-vis the subordinate. Under the accepted theory of appraisal, the latter should be encouraged to enumerate his own faults and successes – and to say what he will do to improve his failings. If that doesn't place the boss in the driver's seat, nothing will.

AQL/AOQ – Acceptable quality level: in SQC (statistical quality control) the limit of defects per 100 units that will be permitted to result from manufacture. The ZD or zero defects approach postulates that no defects is the only AQL – and in practice the best firms, notably in Japan, have raised AOQ, or average outgoing quality, so near to perfection as to make no difference. (*See also*: SQC; Zero Defects.)

ARBITRAGE – The greatest game in town, but not an easy one to find. Where the same thing is selling at two different prices, the smart businessman – thus turning himself into an arbitrageur – buys and sells the same quantity of the currency or whatever at the same time, taking his profit from the price difference.

The most common form of arbitrage is where interest rates differ markedly, say, between two countries. If you borrow in the low-interest country and lend out the money where interest is higher, the discrepancy flows throughout as pure profit. That's so-called "simple" or "one-point arbitrage" – although the transaction may sound anything but simple: for instance, if it involves a currency dealer who really wants French francs for dollars, but finds that he can get a better price if he sells Swiss francs; so he buys Swiss francs with his dollars, changes them for French francs – and ends up ahead of the game.

A "compound arbitrage" can go to two points, three points or even more – for which the type of mind that can cope with three-dimensional chess comes in handy. Less convoluted brains are well advised to keep a sharp lookout for exploitable price discrepancies in any kind of market: for instance, when a predator is hunting the shares of some unfortunate company, and an equally predatory "merger arbitrageur" buys a line of shares in the expectation of a rapid jump. Such jumps may be the key to a fortune – simple or compound.

ARM'S LENGTH – One of the most important distances in management, but also a notoriously difficult one to measure. Technically, it's the quasi-legal term for conducting a negotiation as if the two parties had no other connection with each other – even though they have: for instance, when a corporation buys another business in which its chairman has a financial interest. If it isn't an arm's-length transaction, the shareholders may be robbed.

The catch, obviously, is that somebody has to decide how long that arm actually is – and if that somebody is a crony of the chairman's. . . . Such events, though, require use of arms and their lengths less commonly than relations between two divisions of the same company. To achieve fairness in matters like transfer pricing, the divisions are told to negotiate at arm's length. That's meaningless, however, unless one side is free, say, to take its orders elsewhere, while the other is free to refuse to supply. If not, the arm's length is as illusory as in the case of the chairman's crony. (*See also*: Transfer Pricing.)

ASSET MANAGEMENT – Every business has assets, but not every business manages them – that is, ensures (a) that it only owns those assets necessary for the continuing activities of the corporation, and (b) that the assets are utilised to the optimum level (i.e., expensive plant must not sit idle for half the day).

In its most dynamic form, asset management is a powerful method for keeping overheads down. Nothing inflates a company's fixed costs more than idle plant (see above), or too much property, or superfluous inventory. Good asset management ensures that a company always has what it needs for the job, but never has much more than it needs – still less assets (like shooting lodges or yachts) that it doesn't need for productive purposes at all.

The term can easily be confused, though, with the management phase, very popular in the 1960s, on which Peter Drucker has rightly poured scorn. The "asset managers" of those days didn't manage the assets of acquired companies at all – they sold off non-yielding or low-yielding assets, and thus raised overall returns, while "liberating" large amounts of cash. What those earlier "asset managers" mostly couldn't do was manage the assets that remained. And that proved to be their undoing.

ASSET STRIPPING – Asset stripping is the pejorative form of asset management. While the object of the latter is to reduce the fixed assets employed in the business to the minimum level consistent with its effective operations, the asset stripper is interested only in recovering the cost of an acquisition by selling off anything he can. If that means the total breakup of the company, so be it.

The fate of being stripped is only likely to affect companies whose managements haven't managed either the assets or the operations effectively, so that the market value of the business falls below the market value of its parts. They can also fall victim to purchasers who are not straight asset strippers, but know a bargain when they see one.

Asset strippers realise the bargain by selling off unwanted assets (property, businesses, etc.) for cash and thus reducing the net cost of the total acquisition. If they're lucky, and the original seller is shortsighted, these strippers can ultimately get the core business for practically nothing – which makes it much, much easier to earn a decent, if not a substantial, return on the capital employed. (*See also*: Asset Management.)

ASSET UTILISATION – The acid test for asset management. The more effectively operating assets are used, the more profit (other things being equal) will be earned by the company. You measure utilisation as "asset turnover" (sales value divided by total operating assets), or in sterling terms – pounds of sales per pound of assets. If a business has more in assets than it has in sales, then (in nearly every case) something is very wrong.

ATTENDANCE BONUS – In theory, coming to work on time on every working day should be part of a normal working routine. In practice, absenteeism has become one of the largest involuntary costs in modern industry – many of whose workers are affluent enough to stay away, without suffering much monetary pain, when they feel like it. The disease is immune to normal methods of treatment: but bribery works wonders.

In its simplest form, the attendance bonus is just that: a relatively small sum paid for each day of attendance and forfeited by absence, usually for whatever reason. Many variations are possible. For instance, one company runs a profit-sharing scheme at a straight 10% of pay for each worker. The days of absence are deducted from the profit share; there are few absentees.

ATTITUDE SURVEY – How employees feel about the company and its management is evidently a fact of fundamental importance. Until recently, though, it's been less a fact than a mystery. Now progressive companies carry out attitude surveys on a regular and continuous basis as a vital check on their employment practices.

The technique is very similar to that used in market research studies of consumers (which may also be called attitude surveys, in fact). The basic tool is a questionnaire, which can be supported by deeper interviews to fill out the picture. Because of the Hawthorne Effect, the process of making the survey alone will improve morale. That, however, is only one object of the attitude survey.

Overall, its purpose is to show management how effective or ineffective its human relations policies are, and to indicate where they can be improved. Effective is the word: surveys taken in many companies have confirmed the overriding wish of employees to see the company managed firmly and decisively. Which rubs in the most crucial point about these surveys. If management isn't going to act on their results, there's no point in wasting money on them. (*See also*: Hawthorne Effect.)

AUDIT – The familiar concept of having accountants go through the books to make sure that the company's finances and financial management are in good order has been extended into many other areas of company life. The principle is that of systematic investigation by outsiders (or insiders who are not connected with the operation being audited), culminating in a report on what's been discovered.

At one extreme, the principle has given birth to the "social audit", in which auditors examine, not the business performance of the company, but how well it performs in society at large. At the opposite end of the spectrum, nearest to the familiar financial auditors, are the internal auditors. They monitor what's going on inside the company – not just accounting systems but all systems and procedures – and are no use unless they are both impartial and fearless.

To ensure that they are both, internal auditors often report (which is the only course that makes sense) straight to the chief executive. As an extension of his office, as his eyes and ears, they are invaluable. Their work, of course, is continuous. But there's also a place for one-off audits: the management audit has come into increasing use as the pace of change has forced companies to look at their organisation structures more frequently and more carefully to ensure that they haven't become obsolescent.

The management audit, usually conducted by management services people, looks at the lot: from the overall management structure to the detail of executive development and deployment, from the decision-making machinery to the way decisions and everything else are communicated round the company. Whether or not a wholesale management audit is necessary, and whether or not a full internal audit team exists, no company of any size can afford not to ask the questions the auditors pose – and it must get the right answers. (*See also*: CEO.)

AUFSICHTSRAT – A German word for "supervisory board". It's relevant to British management because of the principle it enshrines: that of the "two-tier board". The supervisory directors have no direct responsibility for management at all; that rests entirely with the *Vorstand*, the management board.

But the latter are all appointed by the *Aufsichtsrat*, which fixes their pay, monitors their performance (to the extent of demanding and getting any information it wants), and can throw out the

Vorstand, or any of its members. The answer to the crucial question of who controls the controllers is clearer under this system than under the American one, where non-executive directors and board committees are supposed to do the same job at arm's length from the executive. The arms, though, are a good deal shorter than they are in Germany.

AUTOMATION – The word given currency by John Diebold in 1952 has been ringing round the world ever since. But only now – after three decades – is Diebold's picture of the fully automated, flexible manufacturing system becoming reality. It took all that time for the technology, the technique, and the acceptance to catch up with the concept.

Diebold didn't invent the word – that was done by D. S. Harden of Ford Motor in 1935. While Harden had not the faintest idea of the shape of things to come – i.e., the computer – he did appreciate the difference between mechanisation, in which manual processes are taken over by the machine, and automation, in which the machine or machines do their tasks under automatic self-adjusting control without the intervention of a human operative.

The distinction didn't seem especially clear until the advent of the computer: in the electronic era, communications, computation, and control have become established as the famous three Cs of true automation. In the hierarchy of CNC (computer numerical control), FMS (flexible manufacturing system), and FMC (flexible manufacturing complex), the Diebold vision has reached its realisation. Any manufacturer who hasn't grasped the significance of automation's coming of age won't, before too long, have much else left to grasp. (*See also*: FMS/FMC.)

AUTONOMY – Once confined to the upper reaches of management theory and practice, the concept of autonomy has now moved right down the scale. Higher up, it still has the same meaning, but vastly greater importance. The autonomous operation or unit, with a responsible manager taking all the operating decisions, has become the basic building block of modern organisational design.

The unit boss is still said to have autonomy, even though key decisions (on top appointments, say, or capital investment) are reserved to the centre. The principle is that only those powers which cannot justifiably be moved out to the periphery will be retained centrally. However, there's no point in pretending that conflict between autonomy and control doesn't exist: the tension is built in, and the object of good management is to make it creative.

Further down the organisation, autonomy changes its meaning – as in "autonomous work groups". What these have is not power, but independence, in the sense that they determine their own work speed, organise their own roles within the group, and so on. The two definitions of autonomy link in motivational theory – which holds that a sense of "ownership" of work increases pride and effort. It's hard to run a company these days without autonomous management groups: but running them with autonomous work groups isn't easy, either, which is why their use is still largely experimental – but worthwhile, all the same.

B

BACK-SELLING – A marketing term for leading the horse to water and making it drink. Using all the means at their disposal, the prime manufacturers (a synthetic fibre company, for example) promote the charms of the end-products which use their goods (an imitation angora sweater, say). The ultimate consumer demand created by this aggressive marketing forces the prime manufacturer's direct customer to buy more of the material or whatever: and both live happily ever after, or at least until the next promotion.

BALANCE SHEET – This basic documentation of corporate finances looks to be essentially a static object. It portrays the state of affairs on a given date, as if the corporation had been fixed in amber – although it does so on the assumption that the business is a "going concern" that will live to fight another day.

To the eye of the true expert, though, the balance sheet is anything but static. To such a virtuoso, the necessary balancing out in the sheet (with the assets on one side equalling the liabilities, provisions, capital, and reserves on the other) is immaterial. He looks for dynamic changes between two consecutive balance sheets, and can also spot – or sense – dynamic events from relationships inside the balance sheet figures.

Some companies make the balance sheet approach dynamic even in less artistic hands. They make profit centres work to monthly balance sheets, as well as profit-and-loss accounts, so as to rub in the fact that the questions of how the business is financed, and how much its value increases, are fundamental to the business of management. Used that way, the seemingly static balance sheet is dynamic. (*See also*: Going Concern.)

BATCH PRODUCTION – Producing a relatively small run of the same product before switching to another run, or batch, of something different. The alternative names, "intermittent production" and "lot production", also give a clear image of the nature of a process that has dominated most manufacturing employment in the era of the assembly line, the age of continuous or flow production – though it's the assembly line that's had all the publicity, most of it bad.

In contrast to mass production, with the production process broken down into elements repeated endlessly on machines capable of only one operation, batch production depends on machines with wider capability – but inherently worse economics. At least, that was the case before improved methods of organisation like group technology came along to alter the balance of costs – sometimes dramatically. (*See also*: Group Technology.)

BAYESIAN THEORY – Following the Bayes rule is one of the basic notions in applying mathematical theory to management problems. Put baldly, Bayes lays down the common-sense principle that, if you have alternative choices, you take the one where you expect the highest payoff – meaning that you must previously have assessed the payoff or outcome for all the alternatives.

Leaving aside the question of what kind of manager would choose anything but the best expectation, the principle is a clear guide to action when (as must be the case in considering the future) outcomes are uncertain, variables are plentiful, and the decision maker is doing the only thing that's possible – the best he can.

BCG – Boston Consulting Group. It's not often that a management consultancy, let alone its initials, wins fame. But BCG did just that because of its brilliant promotion of a matrix approach to corporate strategy – its idea being that companies should grade their various businesses (or products) according to relative market share and the growth of that market.

The matrix puts in the top left square a business or product in a high growth market (over 10% per annum) where its share is at least half as great again as that of the three largest competitors put together; it ranks as a star. With that same share, but in a market growing by less than 10%, it's a cash cow. A smaller share (less than one and one half times the three biggest rivals' sales) with high growth is a "question mark", while a "dog" combines low share and a slow-growth market.

BCG went on to lay down broad strategies for all four categories: (1) invest heavily in a star; (2) invest no more in a cash cow than you need to maximise its cash yield; (3) try to develop a question mark into a star; (4) get rid of the dog. It's an excellent way of taking a hard look at a business. But because no two situations are exactly alike, it's not a particularly good way of either arriving at business decisions or managing the businesses – whether stars, cash cows, question marks, or even dogs. (*See also*: Corporate Strategy; Cash Cow.)

BEDAUX SYSTEM – This incentive scheme is less important for its detailed working than for the principle it enshrines. Charles Eugene Bedaux, a French-born American, favoured paying an incentive bonus for time saved (i.e., the difference between the standard time allotted for a certain amount of output and the actual time taken).

The difference between his scheme and others, though, is that the direct worker receives only 75% of the standard time rate per unit of time saved. The other quarter is divided among the indirect workers in the plant – and that's the eminently correct principle which Bedaux highlights. Not only is it fair that all workers should share in the fruits of better performance, but experience and experiment have shown that productivity of direct workers rises faster when indirects also share in the rewards.

BENCHMARK – In all management, to measure is to know; not to measure is to be ignorant. But the measure is useless unless a standard of comparison is available – a benchmark. The word comes from the past of surveying: the surveyor measuring heights would fix on one point whose height he knew exactly and mark it with a sign that looked like a bench; all other heights could then be evaluated by reference to the one marked.

The problem in management is to select the appropriate height – that is, the standard which you wish to attain or surpass. Interfirm comparison is one approach – you compare the performance of your operation with that of other companies in similar lines of business. Historic comparison with your own past performance is another approach. Or you can settle arbitrarily on a satisfactory number – as in selecting a hurdle rate for investment projects (which is another kind of benchmark).

The benchmark, though, needn't be a high standard, which is to be surpassed if possible. It can be just a fixed point for comparison of like things – as in job evaluation. But evaluation is the key word – and to evaluate anything, you must have standards. The only difference is that, where the standards of the surveyor don't change, those of the manager should vary often – and always upwards and onwards. (*See also*: Hurdle Rate.)

BEST WORLD, WORST WORLD – A simple form of scenario planning. You ask, What's the worst combination of circumstances that could reasonably be expected to affect or afflict my business? And what's the best set of circumstances that could reasonably be expected to prevail? If coping with either Best World or Worst World threatens grave problems (shortage of production capacity at one extreme, say, or an unbearably heavy drain of cash on the other), you take what action you can to forestall the threat.

Beware, though: the middle state between Best and Worst isn't necessarily more probable than either, and disaster may follow if you assume that Middle is most likely and act accordingly. (*See also*: Scenario Planning.)

BIOTECHNOLOGY – Up-market and excessively fashionable name for good old-fashioned ergonomics. It has now become unusable because of its far more important use as a generic term for the applied life sciences, from synthetic insulin to genetic engineering, from which great wonders – scientific and financial – are sure to spring. (*See also*: Ergonomics.)

BLACK BOX – If you haven't the faintest idea how a piece of equipment works, never mind. Just call it a black box. The term means that you understand what it's for – a computer, to take the most common example. But you don't have to know any more about the machine.

In other words, you bypass the technicalities. The catch is that these days, the number of potential black boxes is multiplying so fast that a manager who relies on this convenient approach may end up without any real grasp of what's happening in the corporation – and with total dependence on the experts who actually do know what's happening inside the black box.

BONUS – Strictly speaking, a bonus is uncovenanted – meaning that it's a discretionary sum paid as extra to individuals, or maybe the whole work force, following a good performance by the individual or a great year for the corporation. The usage, though, has come to cover any cash payment, over and above salary and commission, made to employees in recognition of services rendered.

Far from being discretionary, the sum can be tied to fixed performance levels, or even laid down in a contract – especially one made for a senior executive. In the latter case, the bonus is usually linked to annual profits, a practice that has been widely criticised for making US executives concentrate too much on producing short-term gains at the expense of the long-term interests of the business.

Also, the sheer size of some bonus payments has seemed excessive to critics. The criticism is understandable, given the basic principle of all good incentive schemes – that the bonus should be big enough to be highly sought after, but not so big that it distorts the whole pay system.

BOOK VALUE – Whatever the accounts say is the value of an asset is its value – for accounting purposes. If the book value equals the real worth, that's no more than a rather remarkable coincidence. Normally book value will be the result of original or historical cost less the depreciation charged down the years – but this principle is most unlikely to value the business accurately in the eyes of a purchaser or of the stock market.

At periods of depression on stock markets, great companies are commonly found selling at below book value – because investors don't value their earnings high enough to match the capital worth on the books. The other way round, bidders customarily pay well above book value because they think they can earn adequate profits on the higher sum. They are usually quite wrong. (*See also*: Capital; Historical.)

BOTTOM LINE – The place where the net profits are kept – or at least the place where they appear in the annual report – has acquired almost mythological significance. That's odd, considering that, with the increasing complexity of business, the actual figure on that bottom line often means as much, or as little, as the management decides.

The notion of what is or isn't a profit has been radically changed by developments in tax, markets, investment, and many other fundamental areas of management. The "bottom line", though, has become shorthand for an essential attitude of mind: the idea that if, at the end of the day, or the bottom of the line, the company isn't perceptibly richer as the result of a given course of action, that activity is by definition unworthy and should be brought to an end – and the sooner the better.

The concept is especially valuable as an aid to directing the minds of people whose own targets don't necessarily equate with the bottom line: for example, salespeople. Their targets are customarily expressed in terms of volume. The well-known trap is that they can achieve volume by cutting prices to the point where the bottom line, instead of gaining, actually suffers severely. (*See also*: Profit.)

BOTTOM-UP – An American West Coast invention for participative management, which in theory runs the company from the bottom (the hourly paid workers) upwards, rather than under the normal top-down method, with the bosses laying down the law. The principle is supposed to apply not only to human relations but to working methods. And it's a fact that people's suggestions about how to improve their own work, or even whole corporate activities, are often more valuable than those dreamed up on high. It's also a fact, as the Japanese have shown by the *ringi* approach to decision making, that involvement enhances efficiency.

Also, people are more apt to implement their own suggestions than somebody else's. For these reasons, and for others (like the general appeal of bottom-up in the liberated eighties), elements of bottom-up are now appearing in many former strongholds of top-down, even the car manufacturers. Outside the free-and-easy, non-hierarchical world of the Silicon Valleys, it's harder to apply – but well worth the effort. (*See also*: Participation; Ringi.)

BOULWAREISM – The take-it-or-leave-it approach to wage bargaining. As vice-president of the General Electric Company, Lemuel R. Boulware favoured the tactic of making only one offer – one which management considered fair – and refusing to change the offer unless convinced that it was unfair. The contrast is with the haggling approach, in which management goes on raising its offer until the bargain is struck. After Boulware's time (1956), inflation ruled out his tactic; recession brought it right back into favour.

BRAINSTORMING – One of several once-popular techniques for harvesting ideas, usually for future projects or ventures. The procedure is for those assembled in the session to come up with as many ideas as possible, no matter how far-fetched, so as to arrive at nuggets of gold that would otherwise have stayed unmentioned.

The technique never seems to have worked well, but enshrines some valuable principles:

1. The best ideas may not be the obvious ones – people should be encouraged to look outside the narrow confines of their own job concerns.

2. The sources of ideas shouldn't be limited in any way – you need and must encourage contributions from the widest possible circle.

3. The generation of ideas shouldn't be a highly formal, organised process. In fact, a study of "leaders" and "followers" in the instrument industry shows that leaders are *disorganised* in the idea phase, but highly *organised* when it comes to developing and implementing the idea. With the followers, it's the other way round.

Even so, the brainstorming (or, better, brains trust) approach needs organising itself. Participants should be carefully chosen to reflect different types of expertise and experience. The discussions need to be strongly led, and the session must be followed up by *action* (which in the first instance means detailed investigation of any ideas that look to be worth carrying further). The same approach and the same participants can then be used for further discussion of detailed reports on the most likely-looking ideas.

The technique isn't justified, though, by the old argument that many heads are wiser than one. There's no reason to suppose that many foolish heads will come up with a wiser idea than a few; or one. The better philosophy is that many heads will produce *more* ideas – and also more sources for checking them out.

BRAND LOYALTY – Can be expressed as the percentage of all purchasers of your product who have previously purchased it. The main objectives of all advertising and promotion include establishing and reinforcing brand loyalty, since it is always harder to attract a new purchaser than an old one. Paradoxically, though, converts (as in religion) tend to be keener than those already in the faith. Shifts in brand preference are therefore a very powerful measure of advertising effectiveness.

BRAND PREFERENCE – One of the main tasks of market research is to find out which brands consumers prefer and why. Like much market research, this work is most valuable on a continuous basis – so that the marketer can see how preferences are changing – for instance, under the impact of a new product formulation or a new advertising campaign. Ads that do shift brand preferences are the most successful from the point of view of raising sales (that being the whole object of the exercise), since (as noted above) consumers who change brands appear to be more avid purchasers than those who stick to old favourites. (*See also*: Market Research.)

BREAKAWAY – Some of the world's greatest businesses were founded or regenerated by breakaways before the term was ever used. Thomas Watson, Sr., was a refugee from National Cash Register when he took hold of what became IBM, for example. But what was a rare occurrence in Watson's day – the executive or executives breaking away from a corporate giant to set up on their own – has become commonplace, with IBM itself among the most conspicuous victims.

Given that IBM has nevertheless prospered mightily, victim may not be the right word. The majority of successful breakaways escape either from creative companies (like advertising agencies), where the main asset is talent that can always walk out of the door (often with the clients); or from high-tech firms, whose experts may form innovative ideas that their employer won't look at – even if he gets given the chance.

Often, of course, the employer doesn't. A scientist seeing a crock of gold at the end of the rainbow is as likely as any man to want to keep it all (or as much as possible) to himself. But as the IBM example shows, the creativity unleashed into the marketplace stimulates its overall growth, possibly to the broken-away-from company's benefit – provided, that is, that its own creativity is kept truly competitive.

BREAK-EVEN – If all your costs exactly equal all your revenues, you're breaking even, making neither a profit nor a loss. You can work out the break-even point – where costs match revenues – in terms of either units (so many cars, cameras or cheeses) or sales value. In the first place, you divide the fixed costs by the contribution made by each unit: in the second case, you again divide the fixed costs, but this time by the ratio of contribution to sales income. Break-even analysis is basic to establishing the economics of a business – but it is, of course, utterly useless unless the cost numbers in the sums are correct. (*See also*: Contribution; Fixed Costs.)

BUDGET – Probably the most important single word in business – provided that you don't overemphasise its importance. In historical management, a budget was a fixed, immutable document, laying down precisely who could spend what. In modern management, it's a living thing that doesn't control managers but is used by them as a control. If all that sounds paradoxical, so it should – because a budget has several different vital functions.

To begin with (literally), it's the first, absolutely firm year of a planning period, in which forecast sales for the twelve months ahead are related to the expenditures required to make these sales. Second, it's a target-setting mechanism – because you can hold managers responsible for achieving the figures to which they have *agreed* (for budgets should never be *imposed* from above).

Third, it is a control mechanism, because deviation on either the cost or revenue side tells management what is actually happening, as opposed to what was planned; if the budgeted figures are exactly the same as the actuals, that's nothing but an amazing accident. Fourth, it's a ceiling on expenditure: the budget figures provide an upper limit on spending which managers can't exceed without explanation and authorisation.

The last usage comes nearest to the historical budget. It's the (relatively) fixed point round which the rest of the budget turns – for turn it must. Many companies build rotation into their budgetary systems, adding one new quarter every time an old one is implemented – so that managers are always working to a twelve-month plan. Even if this approach isn't used, budgets should be revised every few months to reflect changes in the real world that invariably won't be according to plan.

Note, however, that changing the figures is only part of the exercise – and the residual part, at that. What matters far more is establishing the reasons for deviation and, much more important still, what the manager is going to do about it. Pressure to make up a shortfall from budget is a powerful stimulus to management, even if the budgeted contribution or profit isn't linked to the manager's remuneration (as it very obviously and easily can be). In this way, and every other way, a budget should be a tool for action – showing where positive change is needed and acting as the benchmark against which positive results can be measured.

One thing, though. Beating the budget by miles may not be good management. It might just be bad budgeting.

BUY-OUT – This phenomenon, which gathered speed amazingly over the seventies and into the eighties, kills two birds with one stone. First, it finds a willing buyer for a company's unwanted subsidiary – a purchaser who (importantly) will keep the business and its jobs more or less intact. Second, it thus offloads those unnecessary bits and pieces with which most companies of any size have lumbered themselves in recent years.

The buy-out is usually "leveraged". That is, the existing management of the business concerned finds only a portion of the money required. The rest is raised in loans at fixed interest – usually arranged by an investment group that specialises in these transactions. The package is carefully designed so that the backers and the buy-out management both get rich if the latter does its job properly.

That works because the loans receive only a fixed sum by way of interest. Any increase in the profits over and above that sum flows straight through to the ordinary shareholders. The arithmetic is so attractive that the demand side of the buy-out boom is bound to stay strong. So is the supply side – which is composed of two things: the smart divestment of businesses that don't fit; and, of course, the less-than-smart diversification that bought them in the first place. (*See also*: Gearing.)

BUZZ GROUP – Just as the name says, it's a group of people who buzz around a subject – some problem or topic that their buzzing is expected to clarify. You could call it a syndicate – but that doesn't sound so busy, or buzzy.

BUZZWORD – Any word or phrase that confers upon the user the aura of being in the know, of familiarity with the latest vogue in management. Often, the buzzword is converted into an acronym – like DEMON (decision mapping via optimum networks). It doesn't matter if the user understands the buzzword, so long as the listener either (a) doesn't, in which case he'll be suitably impressed or (b) does, in which case he'll still be impressed. "Buzzword" is, of course, a buzzword itself.

C

CAD/CAM – "Computer-aided" is to design (D) and manufacturing (M) what the first computers were to a task like running the payroll – an electronic revolution which means that nothing will ever be the same again. The drawings needed for any industrial product or process are now produced far faster, with infinite possibilities of modification and experiment, thanks to the computer's astonishing graphic powers – used in 3-D and in colour.

Even before CAD/CAM reached its present technical brilliance, computer graphics had become indispensable in the car, aerospace, and electronics industries. In electronics, you needed computers and microcircuitry to design microcircuits. In fact, a virtuous circle was completed. The design of circuits that could perform any graphic task on a video display unit (VDU) meant that even more amazing circuitry could be designed, which meant . . . and so on. Wherever it's used (and it's already a multi-billion-pound industry worldwide), CAD/CAM has shortened development times and enlarged the potential of the designer.

But the big economic payoff lies in combining the design and manufacturing processes – the computer, once the drawings are complete, uses them to instruct the machines in their tasks. Not only does this speed up production, but it results in higher quality and is the key to improved flexibility. That's why CAD/CAM will be even more important in the future than in the past. Add CAD/CAM not only to numerically controlled (NC) tools and robots, but to the other building blocks of automation, and you

have an FMS, even an FMC – "the factory of the future". Like
the first applications of the computer in the office, CAD/CAM is
rapidly becoming taken for granted. But it's just the beginning.
(*See also*: FMS/FMC.)

CALL-OFF – Placing contracts for supplies to be delivered over
the next year, say, but only when the purchaser asks for them, or
"calls them off". The practice was well known in the West long
before anybody heard of the Japanese "kanban" system which is
an advanced version of the same principle. Call-off demands
close cooperation and trust between purchaser and supplier – but
that's now recognised (by the wise) as essential whatever system
you happen to be using. (*See also*: Kanban.)

CANNIBALISATION – The greatest risk that lurks unseen when a
company broadens its product line is that sales of the new marvel
will steal – or cannibalise – too many of the sales of the old. This
dread of cannibalising existing products helps explain many a
mystery of commerce – including the failure of US car manufacturers to compete vigorously in the compact and subcompact
markets, and the weaknesses of IBM's PC Jr in microcomputers.
In all such cases, the gains to the producer of a successful
lower-priced line will be vitiated to the extent that it loses sales of
the higher-priced, higher-margin products.

The answer to the cannibalisation problem is that the company
concerned is between a rock and a very hard place. If it doesn't
cannibalise existing sales, somebody else (in the case of cars, the
Japanese) will eat up that segment of the market instead. The
shrewd company looks at total penetration of the market and
overall profitability. If achieving success on both counts involves
eating some of the company's own flesh, then so be it – so long as
the cannibalisation doesn't take too much out of its own hide. (*See
also*: Product Line.)

CAPACITY – How much a firm can produce and sell in a given
period is obviously the root of its profit potential. The extent to
which existing capacity is used has a technical number attached to

it, obtained by dividing the actual number of direct working hours by the standard hours budgeted and multiplying by 100 to get a percentage. (Direct hours are those actually used in making the product concerned.)

Even in continuous process operations, 100% of capacity is rarely achieved. In most cases, the operation falls a long way short of the theoretical maximum, through a combination of human, mechanical, and other failures; besides, it's a foolish capacity planner who would plan for the maximum – that would allow nothing for the unforeseen. But there's no doubt that, whether capacity is expressed in man-hours or units of output or machine hours, the extent to which even an apparently busy factory falls short of capacity working is far greater than the contingency provision.

The reason is the same as that noted by location consultants, who can cite numerous examples of companies that were looking for new premises to accommodate extra production capacity when the existing facilities were perfectly capable of providing all that was needed. Errors of layout, organisation, and equipment commonly result in utilised capacity being less than the firm's capital investment paid for (and should have obtained).

Squeezing out more capacity is part of effective management. But so is reduction of the figure at which capacity utilisation yields a profit. In a competitive world of fluctuating markets, capacity and demand are rarely in balance at once. The name of the game, then, as many recession-hit companies found out after 1973, is to get the break-even point so low that halfway capacity operations are in the black – because any rise in output above the break-even level and towards full use of capacity must yield high profits. (*See also*: Break-even.)

CAPITAL – The one thing that every company has, though often not in large enough measure. Capital is always money, whether or not it's been changed into assets or goods. It represents the fundamental financing in the business, the investment that created and sustained it; and it comes in two basic forms – equity (ordinary shares) and debt (fixed interest stock).

Also, arbitrary lines have to be drawn to separate the capital spending (which is supposed to be permanent) from current (which isn't). Thus capital expenditure or investment is commonly defined as spending on an asset with an expected useful life of more than one year – meaning buildings or capital goods (plant and equipment expected to last).

That definition excludes spending on R&D, which may be nonsense in the case of a gee-whiz electronics company, whose exclusive technological prowess is saleable, indispensable – and which, if its useful life doesn't exceed one year, isn't any use. But it's risky not to charge R&D against profits, because that can give a false picture of the business.

The distinction between capital budgets and other spending, though, has become less useful with the increasing importance of non-capital expenditure. Many boards of directors confine their scrutiny to all capital spending over a certain size, while ignoring other cash outflows that are in total far above that level – but are classified as current. You need a capital budget, however, to be sure that, over the years covered, you can find the funds required. This may, of course, mean making a capital issue or two to raise more money from the hopeful investors.

CAPITALISATION – Every firm has capital – either in the form of ordinary shares, or in the combination of ordinary shares and long-term debt. It's possible to have too much capital, in which case the firm is *over*capitalised. This sounds great – but if the capital exceeds the uses to which it can be put, the return on capital won't be adequate, and problems will follow, not least with the shareholders.

The problems of overcapitalisation are easier to solve (by reducing the capital in the business) than those of undercapitalisation. The equity capital must be enough to support the level of trading. If it isn't, the cash required will have to be found elsewhere – usually from the banks. They, alas, are in the habit of charging for their loans. The interest may add significantly to the cash flow difficulties that made recourse to the banks inevitable in the first place. It's a vicious circle from which few escape.

CAPITALISE – The sale for value of future income for capital is a frequently used device and does nobody any harm, unless the future income has been sold too cheaply. But a company can also capitalise not income but expenditure. For instance, companies have elected to treat R&D not as a cost taken against that year's profits but as an addition to the company's capital worth – because the R&D spending will result in valuable patents or in future streams of income.

Another such use of capitalisation is to treat interest payments – on money borrowed by a property developer, say – as part of the equity being created in the building. All such devices give a false picture of current profits and impose a charge on future ones – when earnings may not prove high enough to carry the burden.

Yet another form of capitalisation, and by far the most common, is the scrip issue, when the board decides to divide the existing units, distributing new shares to the holders in a chosen ratio – commonly 1 for 1, or 1 for 2. This is usually hailed with loud cries of delight by shareholders who find themselves holding 2,000 shares where they previously held only 1,000. The company has turned retained earnings into capital – but those earnings already belonged to the shareholder, who is no better off for the exercise. (*See also*: R&D; Equity; Retained Earnings.)

CAREER CURVE – A complex method (also known as the maturity curve) of deciding what people's salaries should be. Suppose that the career concerned is that of a production engineer. After recording the salaries of all production engineers in the firm, plus a chronological factor (age, years since taking degree, years employed as production engineer), you can establish the pattern or distribution of salaries for each year.

Now you can draw a career curve for, say, all those paid in the 70th percentile (meaning that their salaries are higher than those of 70% of other production engineers). Simply look at the salary for his age and his percentile and you know how much to pay the production engineer in question. He may leave, all the same.

CASE STUDY – The most famous method of management education of the business school variety – made famous by its use to the Harvard Business School. Critics argue that the method is purely academic: the case is drawn from real-life business history, its exposition by the faculty is often brilliant, and the task of working through the case and arriving at one's own solution stretches the student's mind – but it's strictly a classroom exercise, and in no sense a preparation for the real thing.

The opposite extreme is "action learning". Even the most ardent devotee of the case-study method should now agree that it needs plentiful supplementing with doses of real life in real time before the student is ready to be a manager – let alone a businessman. (*See also*: Action Learning.)

CASH COW – Of all the definitions in the Boston Consulting Group matrix, cash cow is the one that's liable to last longest. It describes the business that is still generating cash – and profits as well – but is unlikely either to grow much or to yield a worthwhile return on new investment. The chosen strategy is therefore to "milk" the business, squeezing out the last drop of cash as it slowly progresses towards, the end of its natural life.

The trouble with this approach is that it can easily become a self-fulfilling prophecy: starve the cow of investment, and deprive the farm managers of any incentive to improve the herd, and sure enough, the milk, one day, will dry up. There are many examples, though, where one man's cow is another man's star. Tie any label on a business, and one thing's certain: opportunities will go begging. (*See also*: BCG.)

CASH FLOW – Like good health, a positive cash flow is something you're most aware of when you haven't got it. Technically, cash flow comes in two forms – in and out. But since neither has much meaning without the other, cash flow has come to stand, in its widest usage, for the relationship between in and out: that is, the movement of cash from and to the company as bills, wages, etc., are paid on the one hand and customers settle up on the other.

If "in" always exceeds "out" (a positive flow) the company has no worries except where to invest the surplus. The other way round (negative cash flow), the problem will be financing the difference. If you haven't got, or can't beg or borrow, the necessary money, the bills and the wages can't be met – and the company's broke. Actually, that's a far more common cause of bankruptcy than making a loss.

Negative cash flow needn't mean disaster or mismanagement, though. Far from it: a firm that's expanding vigorously and soundly will need cash in large quantities (for investment, R&D, building up production) in advance of receipts. Also, most companies have seasonal patterns – piling up cash in the peak months, running it down in the lean periods. The result will be mounting bank loans – the danger comes when either short-term borrowing or negative cash flow becomes too high in relation to the company's permanent capital.

Cash flow must be used for the microcosm of individual projects as well as for the macrocosm of the firm. In appraising investments or deciding whether to buy a new plant, wise firms look at the net cash flow expected from the project (perhaps on a discounted cash flow basis). On rare occasions, these forecasts of costs against income, period by period, over several years actually prove right – although, since almost nobody ever checks up, who knows? Still, the analytical effort is essential, not to tell the future, but to guide the judgment.

There's yet another form of cash flow: the gross variety. GCF is the sum total of depreciation plus whatever's left from net profits after paying the shareholders a dividend. It measures the internally generated funds available to finance the future – and you don't need a crystal ball to forecast that future if the gross cash flow isn't high and rising. The dividends should be, too, of course. But that's another story. (*See also*: DCF; Depreciation.)

CCA – Current cost accounting: the alternative to historic cost accounting, the traditional method. It's the attempt in inflation accounting to represent the profits and finances of the company in actual, real terms by converting the historic costs in the balance sheet to present-day numbers – or current cost. The only trouble is that the accountants can't agree on how to do this form of accounting, and the managers don't know how to use it. Nor does anybody else. (*See also*: Inflation Accounting.)

CEO – The necessity for the label of chief executive in the US arose from the increase in scope of the modern corporation. In earlier times, one man could combine all the functions of the top echelon of management (or thought he could). Today, a clear split is often considered necessary between the powers of the chairman (ultimately representing the interests of the shareholder) and the managing director (heading up the executive).

Since this isn't always the case, it's helpful to outsiders (if to nobody else) to know that so-and-so is chairman *and* chief executive, while such-and-such isn't. Such-and-such may well be known inside a US company as "chief operating officer" – a common term which, perhaps because it abbreviates to COO, has never caught on in the popular imagination. Also, there's a clear implication that a CEO's COO does a fair amount of fetching and carrying for the American company's most influential executive.

But that's the vital phrase. Behind the initials lies the powerful idea that any organisation, no matter how democratic, must come to a peak – that there must be a single fount of ultimate decision and authority. Without that, the company will find it impossible to develop clarity of objectives or force of direction.

Another factor is that the position of chief executive recognises an inescapable fact of life in larger corporations: a fact no less fundamental for being largely unacknowledged. The "executive" is a formidable body in these organisations, whose destiny lies largely in its hands. One member of the "executive", with a relative handful of shares, may have more influence on what actually happens than the largest single stockholder.

The chief executive is very explicitly (to steal a Mafia term) the *capo di capi*, the executive of the executives, leading them, coordinating their efforts, responsible for their success or failure. It follows, though, that somebody has to ensure that the executive doesn't become a real management Mafia, running the corporation solely for its own advantage. Which is where the non-executive chairman and the board come in – or are supposed to. (*See also*: Chairman; Objectives.)

CHAIRMAN – The chairman may be God in the company – but technically he's only the leader of the board of directors, responsible with them to the shareholders for the proper conduct of the company's affairs by the management – of which the chairman doesn't have to be part. In the old days, the distinction hardly mattered, because the chairman was almost certainly chief executive – whether or not the latter title existed formally, and whether or not the chairman actually concerned himself much with the management of the firm.

In more recent times, the combination of the two roles has come to seem inappropriate. The chief executive has a distinct responsibility, for the management of the corporation; the chairman, as head of the board, is the chief executive's boss – the ultimate control over his activities. If the two jobs are combined, the chief executive has to sit in judgment on himself – either an uncomfortable position, or too comfortable a position, depending on which way you look at it. (*See also*: CEO.)

CHANGE AGENT – Modish term for anybody whose role in some management development programme, or possibly in some wider corporate context, is to facilitate change. The consultants who are often called in to mastermind such programmes like the phrase, because it sounds positive, dynamic and terrifically helpful – and plays down the fact that the consultants are telling other people what to do.

Behind the modishness, though, lies the reality that change, and the acceptance of change, have become vital to success in the modern corporation – and that the traditional difficulty of achieving change, especially in the large organisations that dominate the economy, is now an intolerable burden that must be removed. It's even argued that every good manager must be a change agent – and, if you think about it, the argument is right.

CLOSED-LOOP – A control system is closed-loop if whatever's happening in the process being controlled is continuously monitored. The feedback of information about any discrepancy between what was supposed to be taking place and what actually is occurring (that is, deviation) triggers off corrective action. Indispensable in automated factory operations, closed-loop controls are in principle also applicable to human management.

In fact, all management control systems are theoretically closed-loop. The three-part theory of (1) deviation from expected performance, (2) feedback, and (3) initiation of corrective action can be applied to anything from production costs or inventory replacement or order-chasing or sales performance to the operations of an entire division. Flash reports, coming ahead of regular monthly figures, are designed to alert top management to any deviations from planned performance in time for effective response and repair to be set in motion.

In its most sophisticated form, the approach is known as "management by exception". However, since human beings are not machines, and human failures are subject to differing explanations and interpretations, the closed-loop system doesn't and can't work as reliably in management as in a chemical plant or a machining centre. What managers must have, though, are the key elements of the system: (1) the sensors that measure what's going on in every area, (2) the feedback to ensure that the measures are reported to the people who need to know, and (3) the "comparator". This technical term means anything, from a management accountant to an electronic marvel, that compares actuals with standards and plots the variance.

The fourth element in the chain, though, is what makes the first three worth having. That's the taking of urgent, intelligent action to ensure that what's going wrong is rapidly put right. Since that's the tough part, it's the one that's most neglected. So you get control systems, often very expensively maintained, that actually don't control much. Where that's the situation, if the loop isn't closed, the business may have to be. (*See also*: Management by Exception, Management Accounting.)

CNC – Computerised numerical control is what you get when the automatic, tape-controlled operation of a machine is taken over by a computer. By making the operating decisions, the computer brings the process much closer towards the total automation of the factory of the future. CNC is now the basic element of much modern manufacture – and is spreading fast. (*See also*: Automation; FMS/FMC.)

COACHING – Not the same as training, but an invaluable adjunct to it. As part of his normal job, the boss is supposed to bring out and develop the qualities and skills that his subordinate will need, not just to perform his current job better, but to take on a higher position later on. Coaching is integral to management development, in theory. In practice, it isn't as powerful as it should be, largely because too many bosses forget that coaching is something they're supposed to do. (*See also*: Management Development.)

CO-DETERMINATION – One of the founding phrases in the movement towards employee participation. The principle of co-determination, that embodied in the West German laws on *Mitbestimming*, is that of consulting the work force in advance of decisions, so that the latter can be taken jointly. The mechanism, as in Germany, is formal – usually a system of works councils.

The joint decision making is obviously more apparent than real on matters of most concern to management – that is, the investments, products, marketing, and planning of the firm. Maybe that's why the softer, more noncommittal word "co-determination" came into vogue. But the influence of councils on matters of most direct concern to employees – especially working conditions – is both apparent and very real. And, of course, once you start on the road to co-determination, you never know where it's going to stop. (*See also*: Participation.)

COLLECTIVE BARGAINING – In normal usage, collective bargaining refers to the almost universal practice of determining wages and other benefits by negotiations between the employer's representatives and those of the union which has bargaining rights inside the organisation – though negotiations may cover a whole industry. Even in non-union firms, however, there's an element of collective bargaining, no matter what kind of internal institution it has. Negotiations with unions have the defect that the latter's muscle depends entirely on the threat of withdrawing labour: strikes. This makes bargaining sessions essentially antagonistic in nature, a problem which devices such as Boulwareism can do little to solve. (*See also*: Boulwareism.)

COLLEGIATE MANAGEMENT – The adjective isn't taken from colleges, but from "colleagues". It refers to the substitution of advice and consent for the order and obey relationship of a standard hierarchy. The most collegiate management of all is a partnership, and collegiate management works by establishing many shifting relationships between "partners" – between people who are not equal in rank or earnings, but are held to be equal in their potential contribution to the success of the organisation.

It's a difficult system both to run and to achieve. But it has become to some extent the ideal towards which progressive companies, especially in the high-tech and information industries, are working – even if they know that, for one reason or other, like the fact that they depend on the driving force of one man who owns most of the shares, they'll never quite get there. (*See also*: Hierarchy.)

COMMITTEE – Whenever more than two people meet more than once for the same designated purpose, that's a committee – and will probably be called one. The more bureaucratic an organisation, the more permanent committees it will tend to form – a large bank could easily have three dozen, from the board of directors downwards.

Proliferation of committees raises two problems: (1) preemption of time – all committees not only take up time in general, but specific lumps of time at that; (2) communication: if each of thirty-six committees communicates with each of the other committees only once a year, you get something like the Tower of Babel – only even less constructive.

The key principles are therefore never to use a committee as a substitute for line authority, which can properly be delegated to one person or two people; and to conduct a periodic housekeeping of committees (especially standing ones) to check that they are truly necessary and aren't just wasting people's time. Of course, you may need a committee to do the housekeeping . . . (*See also*: Line.)

COMMONALITY – The clever firm uses the least number of components for the greatest number of product variants. It thus gets the maximum economies of scale without loss of the variety and differentiation needed for the modern product range – all by the magic of commonality.

In the case of a car company, for example, three apparently quite different models (small, medium, and large) can have 70% common parts among all models. The opportunities for commonality are seldom sought as vigorously as they should be – especially when different divisions of the same company are using similar parts but where nobody has worked out how to bring parts – or heads – together. (*See also*: Economies of Scale.)

COMPANY DOCTOR – A consultant, or sometimes a freelance entrepreneur, who moves into a sick firm and applies his remedies – usually staying on as manager no longer than is necessary to complete the cure. The process of surgery, therapy, and healing is often very similar in broad outline from case to case, even in widely different industries: not surprisingly, since the errors that give companies their ailments are also similar in nature.

It's very seldom that a company doctor can get going without amputating some of the senior appendages who made his arrival necessary. With that done, the corporate physician can set about the three basic tasks of (1) restoring liquidity, (2) improving operating efficiency, and (3) raising morale – certain to have been battered during the corporate decline.

The company doctor expects to be well paid for his ministrations. If the deal includes a fat share option in some undermanaged but technologically fit *wunder*-firm in electronics, the physician can end up as a very rich doctor indeed. (*See also*: Liquidity.)

COMPARATOR – *See* Feedback.

COMPUNICATIONS – A new word made up, for uncertain reasons, to describe information technology. *Comp*uter plus communications. They will do these things. (*See also*: IT.)

CONCENTRATION RATIO – An industry dominated by a few large firms is concentrated – and the degree of concentration can be expressed mathematically: the ratio is generally the proportion of total sales taken by a specified number of companies. Most industries tend towards concentration, which is far harder to legislate or act against (supposing that you wish to) than simple old-fashioned monopoly.

CONGLOMERATE – Few terms of congratulation have ever become terms of abuse so fast. Theoretically, almost every large business is a conglomerate – the word merely means any company that has several different activities with no real relation to each other; or, slightly more narrowly, a corporation organised as a holding company with several subsidiaries in differing lines of business. These descriptions, though, fit GEC, which nobody thinks of as a conglomerate, even though its subsidiaries may be in more different industrial sectors than, say, those of a company like Hanson Trust.

"Conglomerate" became a dirty word because of the failure of its big promise – that of secure super-growth: secure because the conglomerate was spread across a range of industries and markets, super because the (literally) unbelievably clever men in command would manipulate the financial structure of the corporation to maximise the earnings per share that were generated by businesses brilliantly masterminded into maximising their performance.

It didn't work, not because it's impossible to manage diverse businesses (Unilever and Procter & Gamble have done so for decades), but because the conglomerates (a) bought too many bad businesses and (b) often didn't have the faintest idea of how to manage their buys, good or bad. The dogs dragged down the stars, and the magic managers turned not a few stars into dogs.

So the true pejorative definition of "conglomerate" is a corporation put together by people who think that's all there is to management – putting a corporation together. That, everybody should now know, is only the start.

CONSOLIDATION – Linking together the accounts of different companies under the same ownership: in other words, a group (the description that fits most corporations). Because it groups more than one company, probably many, the group is really an individual company itself. So the separate accounts have to be "consolidated" in order that the group can present its own corporate accounts. In the process, some tricky questions have to be resolved – for instance, when a group has affiliates in several different countries, each of which operates in a different currency.

CONSUMERISM – The notion that consumers need defence above and beyond their ability to withhold or transfer their purchases has had considerable influence on management – even though the heyday of consumerist champions like Ralph Nader is evidently a long way in the past. In the present, though, and in the future, manufacturers can never forget that an adverse consumerist reaction may be poison.

Anyway, consumerist pressure has resulted in a great deal of legislation of which managements are obliged to take notice. The ancient doctrine of *caveat emptor* has gone out of the window: the new rule is *caveat vendor* – and the vendor had better not forget it.

CONTINENTAL SHIFT – Sounds like a fairly momentous geological event, but actually describes the 3–2–2 system of working shifts. Each shift works, say, three days on mornings, two on afternoons, two on nights – and then takes three days' rest. The system provides a more varied and socially convenient life than straight nightwork in plants where continuous production is essential.

CONTINGENCY – Contingency planning – determining how to react if certain circumstances which may occur do – is vital to modern management, when the unexpected must always be expected. Allowing for contingencies is an integral part of scenario planning and involves obtaining the answer to the key question, "What if?" At a more everyday level, contingencies are built into much of the bread-and-butter of management: for example, budgets will often include an amount for contingencies. At the even more humdrum level of work study, a contingency allowance of up to 5% is added to basic time to cover the incidentals that are bound to occur. If an allowance for contingencies is ever more than 5%, though, something's seriously amiss with basic controls. (*See also*: Scenario Planning.)

CONTINGENCY THEORY – In contrast to theorists who sought to establish absolute principles of organisation, the most modern school of thought reckons that organisational methods change to suit the technology of production. The researcher and writer Joan Woodward observed from studies of many companies that the structure seemed to change according to what they were making and how they were making it – hence her famous answer to the question, "What organisation's best?": "It all depends."

The most recent developments have certainly supported Woodward's view. The free-wheeling methods (if method is the right word) of firms in Silicon Valley are light years apart from the behaviour of the typical engineering firm, whose labour costs are far higher in relation to turnover and whose research and development expenses are a great deal lower.

Some companies are now recognising the force of contingency theory by setting up development and new venture outfits far away from the main camp and in cheap and (fairly) cheerful premises, where they can follow their own organisational logic and not that of top management. It ought to work – if top management allows. (*See also*: Skunk Works.)

CONTRIBUTION – As basic to management accounting as cash flow is to financial management. Contribution is the simplest measure of how economically a business is performing its primary task of providing goods or services for more than they cost. It's the sales income less the variable costs of the business: that is, those costs (materials, say, as opposed to rent) which vary with the amount of business done.

To find out the profit, the fixed costs or overheads have to be taken into account. But so long as there is a positive gap between income and variable costs, the business concerned is making a contribution (hence the word) to overheads. If it isn't making a contribution, by the same definition there have to be some very convincing arguments for keeping the thing going at all.

Contribution is not only the bottom line in the management accounts, which measure financially the operating results of the business; it provides an invaluable tool for business analysis. Contribution per unit of limiting factor, for example, tells you which product made, say, on the same machine should be given priority. You could easily find that contribution per unit is identical – but if one requires more machine time than the other, it's obvious which you should go for.

The contribution to sales ratio is still more powerful. Divide the contribution of different products (again, the contributions are identical) by the sales and you may find that one is earning twice the amount of pence on the pound. Many companies, even though analysis would throw up many examples of these discrepancies, go on pouring just as much effort and resources into the low contributors as they do into the high. That makes no sense – and no contribution, so to speak, to overall performance. (*See also*: Management Accounting; Cash Flow; Variable.)

CONTROL – Control systems are the essence of management, from a single barber shop to a mighty multinational. The key controls are financial, but control over money is only one of the levers that management needs to exert over the company to fulfil the task of "verifying whether everything occurs in conformity with the plan adopted, the instructions issued and principles established".

That's the definition of control produced by Henri Fayol, the pioneer of what's come to be known as "administrative management theory". Fayol went on to say that control's "object is to point out weaknesses and errors in order to rectify them and prevent recurrence" – in other words, criticism and correction. Having rescued his own French firm from bankruptcy, Fayol was convinced that establishing the correct organisation structure was the key to effective control and thus to successful management. As any corporate finance man will tell you, that's certainly true: the set-up determines the strength of financial controls – for instance, the device of having the divisional finance man responsible to the head office finance function as well as to his own general manager.

But administration isn't the object of the exercise or the name of the game. Good controls are accelerators and steering wheels as much as brakes – enabling the corporation to go faster and more safely in the chosen direction. (*See also*: Corporate; Head Office.)

CONVERGENCE – A word that was first applied in electronics, to describe the coming together of different technologies and products, is now getting a wider meaning as the same technological forces cross the former barriers between whole industries. Thus, car firms had nothing whatsoever to do with electronics until very recently; now Detroit is planning to have as many as seven computers at work in its cars: and it is also applying electronic technology on an enormous scale to improve plant operations – and even to take over those operations.

The narrower electronic meaning of convergence hasn't lost any of its force; in fact, the unstoppable process has been gathering strength as personal computers, word processors, private branch exchanges, typewriters, facsimile equipment, copiers, etc. all come to share common components and technology and to relate more and more closely to each other. The culmination of this march of marketing and technology will be the Office of the Future, although the name needs changing, and soon: the Future's almost here. (*See also*: Office of the Future.)

COORDINATION – Coordination is certainly one of the basic tasks of management. No company can manage without the coordination of efforts by different people and different departments; and few companies get the full coordination they want and need between, say, production and marketing or the labs and the product planners.

For all that, it's often a bad sign when coordination itself becomes a full-time management job. The coordinator is by definition somebody senior to the managers whose efforts he is coordinating, but without line responsibility for the outcome of those efforts. It's a recipe for interference and the diffusion of command. The person in charge should be truly in charge – and his job should include coordinating whatever needs to be co-ordinated. Generally, only uncoordinated companies have co-ordinators. (*See also*: POSDCORB.)

COPARTNERSHIP – An advanced form of industrial democracy, in which the employee, in the act of joining the company, becomes a partner in the enterprise, with an entitlement to part of the profits and a voice in the conduct of the firm. The profit share is paid in addition to normal wages, and the partner status lasts only as long as the employment. Copartnership (or "co-ownership") has worked very successfully in some instances, but requires exceptionally careful management – and, usually, a rich benefactor to get the partnership going by giving away his shares. Such individuals tend to be in short supply.

CORE – The upheaval in corporate strategy in the last quarter of the century has centred around the idea that a business must concentrate, not dissipate, its efforts. The thought isn't exactly revolutionary, but the result is that company after company has sold off unwanted, superfluous activities while reorganising itself round, and bolstering, the "core" businesses.

These are the major activities where the management can see strong market positions and growth potential and therefore wishes to make a long-term commitment of resources. The "core" businesses don't have to be related – they can be as far apart as tights from frozen pizzas. Nor do they have to be the base businesses from which the company grew and which it has had all along.

A management unhappy with the cores after it's thrown away the rest of the apple will go out hunting for more core businesses – acquisitions that fit the criteria laid down in the company's strategy. Of course, it could always grow a new core from within, but that's a far harder trick.

The logic of the core lends itself to strategic management as well as strategic planning. The core business gets (and should, too) a core management, concentrated around and dedicated to the core business, just as the corporate management should be concentrated around and dedicated to its cores. Fundamentally, the concept is yet another attempt to make sense out of the conglomerate. But it's about the first one to make much sense itself. (*See also*: Conglomerate.)

CORPORATE IDENTITY – The total image of the corporation, as perceived by anybody who has dealings with it – customers, employees, government, the wider public, etc. In practice, the phrase is generally associated with a narrower aspect: how the company is perceived visually – through its logo, colour scheme, premises, vehicles, etc.

Because these physical elements are obviously important, corporations have spent a great deal of money with specialists (usually outsiders) in the effort to put across the identity they want. The most successful programme in the world is probably that of IBM, whose logo, design principles, and pervasive blue (actually a fairly recent introduction) definitely reinforce the company's marketing effort and have even won it a nickname: Big Blue. But the basic rule of advertising applies – the product must support the packaging: or else.

CORPORATE STRATEGY – This is the Big One – the ultimate task in an era when operational power devolves to divisions and their sub-units, which leaves the managers at the top with something of a problem. What do they do? In fact, there's more than enough that can be done only from the centre of the firm. But "corporate strategy" promised something far more still: the ability to keep hands-on control of a business even though your own hands are not running it.

As expressed through the corporate plan, the classic form of strategy sets out the objectives to be met over the short, medium, and long terms (one year, three years, and ten years, say), and lays down in detail what business managers must do in order to meet the objectives. The strategy decides which business will be fed with capital, which starved – and which dropped. It indicates where acquisitions will be required, and when new products will have to be created.

The number of issues that must be covered is daunting – one author lists no fewer than eleven key areas for which separate strategies have to be devised: product-market, investment, distribution, financial, R&D, cost reduction, diversification, integration, technological, managerial and product design.

No doubt a really assiduous corporate planner could think of a few others. The attempt to fit the whole corporation and its entire future into a top-down, formal strategic plan has now lost favour, though. What's remained, and in even stronger form, is the highly strategic role of setting guidelines – objectives, principles, and overriding purposes – within which individual businesses can form the individual strategies on which the future truly does depend.

COST-BENEFIT ANALYSIS – In its straight-from-the-shoulder form, cost-benefit analysis makes total sense. The costs of any investment (*all* the costs) are set against the benefits (*all* the benefits) which the company will derive from the expenditure. The vital equation means looking to ensure that all contingent capital and operational costs have been taken into account on the one hand; and that the benefits total, on the other side of the sum, has been properly achieved – with all the savings obtained from, say, shorter downtime or lower scrap rates included.

So far, so good. The catch comes when the benefits, unlike those just mentioned, can't be measured in solid arithmetic. How do you measure the value of happier customers, or more satisfied employees, or a better and brighter corporate image? The sensible answer is that you don't, or shouldn't: you decide on these intangible objectives in their own right – and then you decide subjectively (a) whether you think them worth the coin and then objectively (b) whether you can afford it . . .

COST CENTRE – The comrade-in-arms of the profit centre. The organisational principle is no different: the outfit is divided up into operations or activities that can sensibly be regarded as self-contained; and its management is made responsible for controlling the costs which it incurs according to the budget. All profit centres are also cost centres, naturally. But not all cost centres generate profits – for example, the accounting department itself. That doesn't mean they can't be given financial targets for improvement – they should and must be. (*See also*: Profit Centre.)

COST-EFFECTIVENESS – Often confused with cost-benefit analysis, but not the same thing at all. The principle behind cost-effectiveness is the "biggest bang per buck", i.e., the optimum trade-off between expenditure and results. A perfect illustration is the law of diminishing returns: there must come a point where the expenditure on improving performance still further just cannot be justified in economic terms.

Before it can be judged whether spending is cost-effective or not, however, the manager must know what he's trying to achieve by the expenditure, what alternative methods exist of reaching those goals, and how much each alternative will cost. With that basic information, he can then easily work out which combination of cost and results best meets his objectives.

In contrast, cost-benefit analysis seeks to put a value on all the effects of given expenditure – and is often used to argue that the apparently uneconomic is actually worthwhile. Cost-effectiveness (which is almost a definition of efficient management) is based on the unchallengeable propositions that the worthwhile is always patently economic – and that effective management always favours the most profitable alternative.

The most cost-effective policy of all might seem to be killing two (or more) birds with one stone. Beware, though: unless the objectives really are wholly compatible, the supposedly cost-effective solution may sub-optimise on both fronts. In such a case, the search for cost-effectiveness will prove to be a snare and a delusion. (*See also*: Cost-Benefit Analysis; Law of Diminishing Returns.)

COST LEADER – The old view used to be that price leadership was the summit of market ambition. But in the changed and intensified competitive conditions of the eighties, the "cost leader" has overtaken the old concept. It refers to the company with the lowest costs in a particular industry, market, or product line – the point being that cost leadership gives the company the greatest protection against price wars and the greatest flexibility in face of competitive threats.

The classic example is Commodore, which totally defeated Texas Instruments in the home computer wars as the result of a policy of combining cost leadership with a fixed, relatively low profit margin (16%–18%). This kind of policy forces the cost leader to do without the benefits of the super-profits that low costs can bring. But it also makes penetration, even by so powerful an interloper as TI, far, far more difficult.

COST OF CAPITAL – The overall return that a corporation must make to cover the separate returns expected on the three chief constituents of its capital: loans, ordinary shares, and retained earnings. If the proportions are 30%, 30%, and 40%, and the respective returns X, Y, and Z, you add 30X, 30Y, and 40Z. Then divide by 100 and you have (a) the weighted arithmetic mean and (b) a figure which, if it isn't being very substantially exceeded, is an unmistakable sign of mismanagement.

COST OF EQUITY – The importance of the cost-of-equity principle (meaning that the ordinary shares in the company have a theoretical cost, just as the corporate debt has a real cost in interest paid) has only recently been recognised. The cost of equity is clear when the company raises new money; the cost of the promised dividend at the price at which the new shares are sold is the equivalent of an interest payment.

But a hidden cost exists all the time – what it would cost to service any new equity capital. Because (unlike interest) the dividend has to be paid out of taxed profits, the cost of equity to the corporation is much higher than the value received by the shareholder. But unless the corporation earns substantially more on its capital than the cost of equity, the probability is that the value of the shares on the market will decline – and so will the company. (*See also*: Capital.)

COST-PLUS – Cost-plus pricing adds a fixed percentage to standard costs. It's often used to determine transfer prices between divisions of the same company, where it has some serious disadvantages; and for external pricing, where the drawbacks are worse. They can be still more lethal (as the Ministry of Defence knows to *its* cost) when the cost-plus prices are not based on standard costs – because they can't be, since (typically for a new defence system, such as Nimrod) the costs aren't known in advance.

The cost-plus contract thus guarantees the manufacturer a predetermined profit margin, *whatever the costs then turn out to be*. He thus has no incentive to keep costs from escalating; on the contrary, the higher the costs, the greater his profit. In every country where military production and procurement are important, solving this problem has driven men quietly mad.

Even when costs are known (as in an established programme), cost-plus can open up a trap for the unwary procurer. If costs reduce over time because of the learning or experience curve, the contractor will clean up at the customer's expense. The point is that both costs and prices should be flexible – the first downward and the latter upward – to make the most from modern markets. (*See also*: Standard; Transfer Pricing; Learning Curve.)

COUNTERTRADE – A newfangled word for the very old-fashioned game of barter – in which Company A sells its offerings of X to Company B only by agreeing to accept goods Y as part of the deal. A's problem is then to get rid of Y, which of course it doesn't want, but sells as best it may.

In normal circumstances, nobody would countertrade – thus, if they are doing so, it must be true that the circumstances are abnormal. This is far more likely to occur when a company from the prosperous West is trading with one from a less developed country in the Third World, or a corporation in the Soviet bloc. It's then often a question of countertrade or simply don't trade; and it makes much more sense than bribery, after all. (*See also*: LDC.)

CPM – The critical path method comes into its own with any project, from erecting a building to launching a product. The object is the same as in PERT: to plan the project so that it is completed in minimum time, on schedule, and at budgeted costs. A Du Pont invention, CPM is applied after critical path analysis has found the critical path through a network.

That path is the route through the network that governs the total time taken to complete the project: i.e., any delay along the critical path will cause the whole thing to be late. Unlike PERT (and this is the only significant difference), CPM only considers two time possibilities for activities in the network: "normal" time and "crash" time. Both estimates are costed, and the plan is drawn up accordingly. Actuals are compared with plan, and the project managers can react accordingly, with all the consequences of their decisions clearly mapped out. The critical path is basic to all organised activity, and it's critically important to know where it is and how to find your way along it. (*See also*: PERT.)

CPT/CPM – Cost per thousand is the basic measure of the expense of advertising. It's a simple sum – arrived at by dividing the numbers of people reached by placing an ad in a given medium into the price (rate) charged for the ad. It doesn't always follow that the lowest CPT is the best value for money – but persuading the advertiser otherwise is seldom easy. If you're advertising in the really big leagues, of course, you're only interested in the CPM: cost per million – which will cost you millions.

CREATIVITY -- The ability to produce original ideas that will result in positive benefit to the organisation. The term is in narrow usage in the advertising industry, whose "creative" people write and design the ads, and are seen as a breed apart from the men and women who win and serve the accounts. But in recent years creativity as a buzzword has spilled over into the management world – ever since it became obvious that innovation is increasingly the key to corporate survival, let alone growth.

Fostering creativity, though, is even tougher than fostering innovation – despite the fact that the two are obviously linked. The reason is that innovation can be built into the procedures of the company and will, anyway, mostly stem from its current activities. Creativity, in contrast, may involve the leap into the unknown – and is far more an attribute of the individual mind than a corporate function.

Still, the evidence is that most managers are much less creative than they could be; and several corporations have tried to enhance individual creativity by training sessions in techniques like lateral thinking. The most creative thing most corporations can do, though, is to ensure that the bureaucratic and other organisational barriers to creativity come tumbling down – and that's not easy. (*See also*: Innovation; Lateral Thinking.)

CREDIT – Borrowing – but that's not all. In the first meaning, credit is the lifeblood of commerce, but also the deadly poison of the unwary. The word also (among other things) means an entry made on the right-hand side of the accounts – representing either a debt incurred or an expense undergone; but its main commercial significance lies in the time allowed for settlement of these right-hand entries.

The typical period for trade credit is thirty days. If all credits were settled in the same time-span, there would be a perfect balance. In fact there isn't – because some managements won't settle and others can't. Stretching trade credit is the resort of rapacious big companies and underfinanced small ones, which tend to use it as a substitute for permanent finance. It isn't – as they find out when the trade creditors foreclose.

One group of traders, though, is generally in happy surplus on its trade credit – the majority of retailers who get supplies in credit, but are paid themselves on the nail – except to the extent that they keep the credit merry-go-round turning by advancing credit to their customers in turn. (*See also*: Trade Credit.)

CRITICAL PATH ANALYSIS – *See* CPM.

CRITICAL SUCCESS FACTOR – What a company has to have, or has to do, to achieve success in its chosen sector of the market. Sometimes called KSF (key success factor) or KFS (key factor for success), it can also be applied to individuals (what do they need to do right in order to succeed in their jobs?) – or, indeed, to any project or activity.

The key factor about key factors is that, by definition, they are never the same (except by accident) between one market segment and another. Another vital point is that the whole spectrum of the business has to be examined to establish the CSFs, from the point where everything begins to the point where it ends, with the product or service united with its customer.

Nor does it make any sense to concentrate resources on a CSF which happens to be the opposition's strongest point. An effective search for CSF will reveal a critical area where you can establish a commanding position – and a lasting success.

CURRENT – The distinction between current and non-current is just as basic to a firm's finances as the distinction between direct and indirect (as in direct costs). Current assets are the opposite of fixed assets: the goods moving (you hope) through the warehouse as opposed to standing there. Current covers everything: raw materials, work in process or progress, unsold stock, unsettled bills to customers – plus cash in hand or in the bank account.

Liabilities of the current variety are different from the long-term kind – current means the bank loan due on demand as opposed to the term loan due in five years. The amount owed to suppliers for the current assets is obviously a liability. So are the latest tax bill, the pending dividend – everything that falls due for payment, or which may fall due, within a year.

The ratio of current assets to current liabilities – the current ratio – is less severe than the acid test, which only counts those current assets that can be quickly converted into cash. A very general rule of thumb is that assets should be at least half as great again (50% higher) as the liabilities. If they aren't, urgent current action is required to correct a situation, which, if allowed to develop unchecked, will lead to current disaster. (*See also*: Acid Test; Direct Costs.)

CYBERNETICS – Computers linked with sensors and responding to what the sensors tell them is happening are the realisation of cybernetics. This once-exotic, far-fetched sci-fi field has moved stage centre with the rise of robotics and automated, flexible manufacture (FMS), both of which depend on cybernetics for their foundation. These control systems operate on the same principle, but in brilliant fashion, as the closed-loop system. (*See also*: FMS/FMC; Closed Loop; Robotics.)

D

DBMS – Database management system. The "in" phrase in the area where top management meets the data processing people. The database, potentially among the company's greatest assets, has escalated from the simple meaning of a central file of information (which doesn't have to be in a computer, but probably is) to the core of an MIS, or management information system. In this elevated role, it's an organised collection of the supporting information needed to run the corporation and all its major activities.

Because of the sheer amount of storage and housekeeping required, the database is one of the last strongholds of the large mainframe computer. The minis and micros distributed round the corporation all plug into the database for access to its files – which are so organised that the amount of redundant (i.e. duplicated) information is kept to the minimum.

Obviously, the database is useless unless you can get hold of its contents fast (retrieval) and unless it's updated. The DMS (data management system) is the software that makes these wonders possible. Databases also exist outside organisations, in the form of computerised reference files, some highly specialised, which enable the seeker after truth to find the information he wants – on a whole market, say – and (far more important) to collate the data so it makes usable sense. (*See also*: Distributed; MIS.)

DCF – Discounted cash flow is a sophisticated version of the simple saying that a bird in the hand is worth two in the bush. That is to say, money that you're going to receive in five years' time isn't worth as much as money you can receive now – even if there's no inflation.

The reason? Because between now and Year Five you can earn interest on the money you received. The interest rate gives you the discount factor by which future expected cash flows from an investment can be reduced in value. This provides a more accurate approach to investment appraisal – though that doesn't mean it *is* accurate. After all, anybody who knows what rates of interest will prevail over coming years is in a position to make an easy fortune out of that knowledge alone.

The method is used mostly to compare alternatives when you have a choice between capital projects. You set down the cash flows expected year by year (or the cost savings expected to result from the investment) and discount them by the relevant factor. Thus, if the interest rate you've picked on is 10%, your first-year cash must be devalued by 0.9091; the second year by 0.8264; the third by 0.7513 – meaning that an expected £10,000 becomes worth only £7,153.

That figure is called a "present value". Add up all the PVs for all the years, subtract the capital cost of whatever you're buying, and you've got the "net present value" of your alternatives. Of course, you plump for the one with the highest NPV – and only hope that the calculations don't prove too grievously awry. But never rely on DCF alone when appraising an investment: always look at other measures, too, like payback and return on capital employed. That way you'll get a better picture – and (who knows?) maybe a better investment. (*See also*: Cash Flow.)

DEBT-EQUITY RATIO – The proportion of medium and long-term debt to shareholders' equity is one of the most definitely vital statistics in management. This ratio establishes the degree of a company's gearing or leverage. While it's perfectly possible for a company to be entirely debt free (and such companies are usually extremely strong financially), the use of debt adds a powerful weapon to the armoury.

That's primarily because, as with consumer debt, it enables the debtor to purchase something which otherwise he couldn't have afforded. Provided that the investment financed by the debt produces a yield that is higher than the interest on the debt (interest which, remember, is tax-deductible), there's bound to be a gain in earnings per share.

Which suggests the obvious question of why companies don't borrow up to the hilt. Some do, but their managements often live to regret it; or, to be more precise, their managements often die to regret it. Usually, it's a new, turnaround management that faces the task of "cleaning up" the balance sheet, selling off assets and, if it can, selling more ordinary shares to get the debt-equity ratio right down.

The other way round, as the ratio starts to rise, so does the proportion of the company's profits preempted by interest payments. If there's a recession – in the economy or the company's own business – there may be nothing left for the shareholders: maybe not even enough to cover the interest. In which case the whole company falls into the lap of the creditors.

The classic awful example is Lockheed, which borrowed more than the shareholders' equity to finance the Tristar. When that project chalked up one of the largest losses in aviation history, the company – among the strongest in the United States in many respects – could only escape bankruptcy by turning desperately to Washington for help. If you don't want to do a Lockheed, watch that ratio: in most businesses (oil, property and land are exceptions) 30% is generally thought to be the golden mean. (*See also*: Stockholders' Equity; Gearing; Yield; Earnings per Share.)

DECENTRALISATION – Nearly all corporations are decentralised whether they think so or not – that is, very few major businesses have all their operations under one roof. But not all corporations decentralise power, authority, decision making – call it what you will. It's perfectly possible to hold all the reins at the centre – but it doesn't work perfectly well.

In fact, often it works terribly badly: first, because the centre isn't sufficiently omnicompetent to take all decisions and initiate all actions correctly; second, because robbing people lower down of responsibility also lessens their potential contribution and is an excellent demotivator; third, it tends to make the whole management process top-heavy and cumbersome.

For all these reasons, and others, decentralisation has been the dominant mode for decades now. Its basic concept has often been the profit centre or cost centre: the company is divided into a hierarchy of profit-responsible divisions, subdivisions, and units, each with its own responsibilities, objectives, and budgets. On the marketing side, the equivalent is the brand, with responsibility for performance of an individual brand delegated to an individual manager – in theory.

Most of the above style of decentralisation has been pretty theoretical, in fact. Power got stuck higher up, and very little filtered through. The new vogue is more far-reaching. The idea is to divide the corporation into real businesses, built around their markets; maybe even formed into real companies. Whether or not they have their own boards of directors, these businesses are led by a single responsible manager, given considerable freedom to run them as he likes.

That's the basic principle of the strategic business unit, or SBU. The great attraction is that it makes not only organisational but marketing sense. You can't decentralise to the extent of giving managers a business that's their own. But you can make them manage as if it were – and these days that's vital. (*See also*: SBU/SPU; Profit Centre; Cost Centre.)

DECISION – The most bandied-about word in management in the last couple of decades. One writer has actually said that "the primary task of managers is to make the right decisions at the right time in order to effect change for the purpose of optimising business performance." But there's a confusion here between one-off decisions (do we build this plant, buy this company, launch this product, scrap this department?) and the continuum of smaller decisions, many of them almost automatic, that keep the business alive.

The one-off decision, which can basically be taken only at the highest level of the corporation or unit, is more glamorous. Thus, the group known as "decision makers" – the top management – has the prestige that goes with glamour and power. But the truth is that results in any company also rest on short-term or medium-term decisions taken by people far below these elevated levels.

It's also true that management theory holds that decisions should be pushed down as far as possible, to the level of competence. The same writer quoted above says that "this allows senior managers more time for making decisions of a more complex nature". A more important reason, however, is to place responsibility for decisions as close as possible to the level at which they will have to be carried out. That way, there's a better chance that both the decision and its execution will be of the optimum quality.

Wherever the decision is taken, though, there's a deep, often-buried anxiety in management that the quality of decision taking is poor and could be improved – if only they knew how. Hence the bouts of enthusiasm for scientific or quasi-scientific methods of decision making. They *sound* better than flipping a coin. But are they? (*See also*: Decision Theory; Decision Tree.)

DECISION THEORY – Decision makers who use decision theory are rare animals – but that doesn't mean the theory should be ignored. Fundamentally, it seems to reduce or translate decision making to numbers, so that the option (or "strategy") chosen will be the optimum selection. The decision theorist juggles "states of nature" (the situation as is) to arrive at "outcomes" to which monetary values can be ascribed in a "payoff table".

He is now in a position to establish "expectations": that is, he values each outcome, gives each a probability, multiplies probability by outcome, and adds the whole lot together. Whichever outcome produces the highest score is the one which, if you believe this sort of thing, should govern your choice of strategy. Otherwise you may prefer to follow the advice of a brilliantly successful entrepreneur: "If you have to make complicated calculations to justify a decision, don't take it."

The truly nervous decision maker can put the whole process on a computer. A technique known as the decision table does this for low-level decisions – like stock control or plant operation procedures. At higher levels, the procedure given above can be computerised. But nothing can automate the human brain and will – on which decisions ultimately rest. The most useful role of decision theory is simply to force rational analysis to precede the moment of choice – or truth.

DECISION TREE – The most picturesque of the allegedly scientific aids to making decisions. The analyst charts all the possible outcomes of different options, and charts all the latters' outcomes, too. This produces a series of stems and branches (hence the tree). Each of the chains of events is given a probability and a monetary value.

The completed chains can then be compared, and the most lucrative one (theoretically) gets the prize: being chosen. While the description of consequences is useful, the pretence that the method brings greater precision is not. Neither the probabilities nor the expected values are reliable: multiplying the two together doesn't make good better – it may make bad worse.

DELEGATION – The key to effective exercise of a manager's responsibility has to be passing on that responsibility to other people. But how you delegate, and how much you delegate, involves great skill, self-control, and judgment. Nobody can delegate properly who doesn't understand the force of the ancient maxim that you don't get a dog and then bark yourself.

In other words, if you give a job to somebody, you must (1) define it clearly, (2) get the person to tell you how he or she proposes to execute the task, and (3) let the person get on with it – with reports from time to time on how it's going.

This simple, sage advice was demonstrated in a book that doesn't contain much else, the best-selling *The One Minute Manager* by Kenneth Blanchard and Spencer Johnson. The fact is, though, that most delegators try to do their subordinates' jobs as well as their own, second-guessing and interfering all the way. This pseudo-delegation guarantees that neither job gets done well – that of the subordinate or that of the bumbling boss.

DELPHI METHOD – Delphi was the place where ancient Greeks consulted the oracle who would foretell the future (if, that is, you could correctly interpret what the oracle said). The Delphi method is an up-to-date version, which consults not oracles but experts. Each of the wise men is asked to make a forecast on the subject in question – say, the use of plastics in cars in the year 2000.

All the individual forecasts are collected and summed up; every one of the experts gets a copy of the summary, and also gets the chance to change his forecast in view of what the others have said. You go on collecting, summarising, and revising until (since miracles never cease) you have a unanimous prediction.

Whether the view of the future is any better for this elaborate procedure is a matter of opinion, and open to doubt. What is certain, though, is that the Delphi method is unlikely to leave many important stones unturned. Whatever defects the consensus may have, the total scenario through which the experts have worked provides a broad canvas within which, very possibly, the future will actually be painted.

DEM – The idea of "design for efficient (or easier, or economic) manufacture" is so obvious, and so basic to industrialisation, that its neglect in the West is amazing. It took the Japanese example to wake up complacent companies to the truth that good design, while it is ultimately justified by good user response, isn't really good unless it also achieves the lowest possible production costs.

That means, more often than not, reducing the number of parts. For instance, the new Jaguar XJ40 design has only 330 body parts, compared to 560 in its predecessor. DEM also means designing a product so that component manufacture and assembly can be carried out automatically. If it can't, the company will not only be inefficient – it will probably also be uncompetitive.

DE-MERGER – The large-scale version of divestment, disinvestment, or divestitures: when two companies, having joined together in unholy wedlock, are put asunder because it hasn't worked out. There aren't too many examples in business history – not because few mergers have been mistaken, but because it's generally too complex (not to mention shaming) to admit to the mistakes and proceed to unravel them.

DEMON – For those who are keen on scientific methods of taking decisions, DEMON is the very devil. It stands for Decision Mapping via Optimum Networks. To be precise, the networks are "stochastic" (i.e., random) decision trees. They'll help you decide whether to take a new product on to the national market based on the test market results. (*See also*: Decision Tree.)

DEPARTMENTALISATION – How a company is divided up, or departmentalised, is obviously one of the basic factors in its organisation – but it is also, less obviously, fundamental to performance. You can adopt many different approaches – the Army traditionally uses departmentalisation by numbers: so many men to a company, a platoon, etc.; shift work departmentalises people by time. Very commonly, companies are divided by function: the marketing, personnel, production, finance departments, etc.

Along with territorial division (by county, town, etc.), functional departmentalisation is the oldest and most traditional form of organisation. However, tradition has been widely abandoned, mainly in favour of product departments – organised around a particular product or product line. Other firms organise by customer (by industry – or by size, say, with large, medium, and small customers being served by different parts of the company).

Customer departmentalisation is very similar to, but different from, division by market – in which a company may split up its efforts among the schools, hospitals, and office markets, for example. Then there's the very common division of a plant among the various types of production activity that it contains, and also the separation of a company into departments simply according to where its plants happen to be.

This approach is now thought to be suspect: many companies prefer to divide by both plant and product, dedicating one facility to one product, and only one. Also, combining more than one form of departmentalisation is now widely favoured as the best way of combining the main advantages of different forms of organisation while minimising the disadvantages to which all are subject. (*See also*: Functional; Matrix.)

DEPRECIATION – Nearly all fixed assets depreciate – that is, you can't sell them for as much as you paid. For accounting purposes, though, you have to work out how much depreciation has taken place each year. That's an arbitrary or theoretical figure, concrete only in one sense: that the tax man accepts the reduction in profits (and thus in tax) which results.

The accountants can choose between straight-line depreciation, in which you reduce the value of the asset by the same amount each year (say, £100,000 on a £1-million asset); or the declining balance method, with a fixed percentage lopped off annually. These days, the bigger the percentage, the better – because the rapid pace of obsolescence makes traditional depreciation periods obsolete, too; and there's a built-in reluctance to scrap machines that aren't fully depreciated. Spare the depreciation, however, and you could spoil the whole company.

DESK RESEARCH – An amazing amount can be discovered about any industry, any market, without ever leaving your desk. The information explosion has produced an embarrassment of facts and figures about almost every human activity. Desk research, which is relatively cheap and easy, is the indispensable preliminary to other investigations in market research. But it's unwise to pin all your hopes on the Desk.

DILUTION – The technical term for what happens in an acquisition if the purchaser overpays for the purchased company in shares. The ordinary shares in issue rise by the number paid out for the acquisition, but the earnings don't rise in proportion. Consequently, earnings per share for the existing shareholders are lower than they would have been but for the acquisition.

Studies have shown that in perhaps half the cases of major acquisitions, the original shareholders are still worse off years afterwards than they would have been had the deal never taken place at all. The reasons are usually mismanagement of the new company, or misjudgment of its value in the first place. Thus shareholders should be wary of applauding any deal that does dilute their earnings – it may prove to be the first step towards de-merger or divestment, when the price obtained for the divested business seldom compensates for the pain inflicted by past dilution. (*See also*: Acquisition; De-merger; Divestment.)

DIRECT COSTS – All costs are direct – in the sense that they all fall directly upon the same cash box. But technically the costs incurred in making a particular item, or providing a specific service, and not in anything else, have to be kept separate from costs that are widely shared.

To spell it out, the labour and raw materials employed are plainly direct costs; the rent of the whole plant is clearly not direct – or rather, it is indirect. All manner of debate has gone on, and will probably continue till the end of management time, over which costs should go in what column, and over just how indirect costs should be apportioned to cost centres; but the debate isn't as vital as the principle of separation.

The point is that the indirect costs are largely fixed. The directs vary with output and efficiency – so that is the number to watch, both as a management control and as a basis for pricing decisions. A "direct", incidentally, is a direct worker (i.e., one whose wages are legitimately treated as direct costs). "Direct labour", though, is something else again – a construction work force that isn't employed, as usual, by a contractor, but which is employed by the organisation putting up the building or whatever.

DIRECT RESPONSE – All consumer advertising is (or should be) aimed directly at the purchaser. But if the latter can respond directly to the advertiser – by returning a coupon or phoning a number – one thing's certain: the advertiser knows exactly what he's paid for. That's why wise advertisers who aren't in mail order (for which direct response advertising is crucial) sometimes include a direct response feature in their ads: to test their effectiveness. Not to be confused with direct advertising, where the ad itself is delivered straight to the consumer – who may complain about it, but who often responds in large enough numbers (2.5% response is a bonanza) to have made some large enough fortunes.

DISCOUNTED GROSS BENEFIT-COST RATIO – Take the present value (that is, the sums as devalued by a chosen rate of interest) of your forecast cash inflows for a project, and express them as a ratio of the PV of the forecast cash outflows. This gives you the so-called profitability index – and is one guide to the question of whether you should proceed at all. (*See also*: DCF.)

DISCOUNTING – The standard commercial practice of discounting for volume – that is, charging less, usually by given percentages, for larger orders – had an enormous impact on retailing when the first shrewd operators, back in the fifties, realised that, by passing volume discounts on to the customers, they could undercut the department stores on consumer durables like TVs and washing machines.

The effects have been seen, not only in the emergence of discounters of all shapes and sizes, but in pressure on manufacturers from large orthodox outlets for greater discounts and other special deals on their own purchases. In fact, several early discounters went broke as their own costs rose in an effort to come nearer to department store convenience and service – an effort needed as the department stores got into the discount game themselves.

The moral of those days still holds good. The bigger the discount to the customer, the lower the gross margin to the retailer (that is, the difference between buying cost and selling price) and the smaller the room for business errors. But there's also a trap for suppliers, too: overdo the discounts, and you destroy the profits – and, in a badly managed company, the salesman clinching the deal by discounting may not have the faintest idea that destroying the profits is exactly what he's doing. (*See also*: Gross.)

DISTRIBUTED – Distributed data processing is the computer revolution nobody predicted; it is the great swing away from a central mainframe computer – containing all the information, and situated in its own temple full of experts and mysteries – towards the provision of easily accessible computing power wherever it's needed in the organisation. The revolution, like some political uprising, began without the knowledge of the ruling class – top management. People in the managerial proletariat surreptitiously installed their own Apples and other microcomputers. Now the revolution is unlikely to end until there's an intelligent terminal on every desk: that is, a machine that can both compute on its own and communicate with the greater power and memory of the mainframe.

DIVERSIFICATION – Managements can diversify a product range, the company's geographical markets, its product markets, or the company itself – in ascending order of risk. Adding to the product range with new variants or new features designed to appeal to new markets is not only sensible, but increasingly essential if the line is to retain existing sales, let alone add new ones.

The further the product is from the original range, naturally, the greater the risk: the newer the product, to the company and the market, the greater the chance of failure. On the other hand, the risks of *not* innovating are rising steeply – and this is one risk no company can afford to run, not today.

You can have your cake and eat it – for instance, when a product like a hand drill is adaptable from consumer to industrial markets by redesigning around existing components. Equally, geographical diversification can produce fairly painless profits, if handled with care. The same range, with or without modification, can be sold in new regions or countries – though it won't be sold successfully unless the management recognises that new circumstances will almost certainly arise.

Going into an entirely different market with an entirely different product is a game fit for heroes: it's possible to win, but not without great effort, and it's entirely possible to lose. That shouldn't, in theory, be the case where the new market is purchased by acquisition of another company. The acquired management theoretically brings the market knowledge whose lack explains so many diversificational failures.

Unfortunately, diversifying the whole company by acquisition or merger is prone to all its own difficulties as well. That's why diversification strategies based on the defensive principle of "not too many eggs in one basket" are inherently less cogent than those based on the positive idea of maximising the company's profitability by finding attractive new market areas.

After all, it's no good having those eggs in several baskets if all of them (eggs *and* baskets) are bad. There's no virtue, either, in having too many eggs in too many baskets. (*See also*: Acquisition; Conglomerate.)

DIVESTMENT – The opposite of diversification, and often its consequence. Companies galore have bought unrelated businesses, often by the dozen, only to find that the low returns on their expensive purchases were dragging down the whole corporation. Conversely, it had to follow that selling the bad eggs, even if the proceeds didn't cover the original book cost of the purchase, would raise overall returns.

"Selling bad eggs", or any other truthful description, doesn't sound too good. Which is where the bland word "divestment" (or divestiture) comes in. The semantics convert actual failure into what sounds like a dynamic, progressive move. But whatever word is used, the policy makes abundant sense. History records many cases of companies that have been brought to their knees by ruinous diversification. It records none of a company ruined by selling off an unwanted and unprofitable asset.

DOWNTIME – When a machine or a line or a computer could be producing but isn't, you've got downtime. There are only three possible causes: set-up or make-ready for a changeover to different work; the regular pause for planned or preventive maintenance; or unplanned breakdown. The difference between an efficient and sloppy plant can usually be seen in the ratio of available machine hours divided by hours actually in operation (i.e., after downtime). It's a statistic that hawk-eyed managers always watch – like hawks. (*See also*: Set-up Time; Preventative Maintenance.)

DUMPING – When a company, foreign or domestic, offloads its product at low, low prices (less, that is, than other existing buyers are being charged), that sounds a marvellous idea – for the luckiest customers. But dumping is a pejorative word, especially in international trade: because the dumped goods are driving out domestic production and jobs. That's why all governments have anti-dumping powers.

One man's dumping, though, is another man's marginal costing. If you're a European steel producer, it makes sense to sell extra tonnage into the US East Coast at lower prices than you charge at home: because the marginal cost of making the extra steel for the United States will be much less than the average cost of output. It's so difficult to prove dumping that very few cases brought against alleged dumpers succeed – not that it makes any difference. A powerful country like the United Kingdom simply finds other ways (like involuntary voluntary quotas) to stop cheaper foreign goods like Japanese cars coming in too heavily.

Dumping investigations can have embarrassing results, anyway, such as the discovery made by many firms that the foreign, usually Japanese competition, is cheaper for the good and simple reason that its production methods are much more efficient and its costs consequently much, much lower.

E

EARNINGS YIELD – The reciprocal of a price-earnings ratio. It tells you how the profits available to shareholders relate to the equity as valued on the stock market. It's an easy sum. Just divide the net income by the current share price times the amount of stock in issue – and multiply by 100.

To spell it out, the company's net income is £5 million. It has 5 million shares in issue, selling at £20 apiece – making the capitalisation £100 million. Divide 5 by 100 and multiply by 100 and you get the answer: 5%. The figure is rarely used in London (and even less in the United States) for two main reasons:

1. It's easier to gauge the degree of inflated esteem in which the market holds a share by saying it's selling at 40 times earnings than to point out that its earnings yield is 2.5% (although the figures mean exactly the same thing).

2. The earnings yield figure relates directly to the dividend yield. If shareholders were to note that there's an earnings yield of 10%, but a dividend yield of only 3%, they might (just might) ask for higher dividends – or even ask what's going on. (*See also*: Net; Capitalisation; Yield.)

ECONOMIC LIFE – So long as an investment is yielding a return, it's economic and has an economic life. Once it ceases to do so, it is technically or at least economically dead. Two points are crucial. First, the effective end of an investment's useful life usually comes well before what you might call the point of no return, when it actually costs more to use than to stand idle – and hanging on to obsolescent equipment, say, can have grave consequences competitively.

Second, however you calculate economic life, it has plainly been getting shorter – often much shorter. Even managers in industries of relatively stagnant technology, like paint manufacture, are replacing plant that lasted fifty years with plant that may not have an economic life beyond two decades – and by the standards of the faster-moving industries, twenty years is practically for ever.

ECONOMIC RENT – Just rent – but the phrase has significance in management because of the practice of charging subsidiaries or profit centres a notional rent that is built into their financial targets. "Economic" refers to the fact that a true market rental should be charged if a true result is to follow.

The desired result is to make the outfit function as closely as possible to a stand-alone business. The exercise is fictitious, but the fiction does contain an important truth – that if the outfit can't cover the real value of the premises it occupies, it doesn't have much excuse for being in business at all.

ECONOMIES OF SCALE – Traditionally, economies of scale arose largely by increasing scale. As the volume of output rose, while the fixed costs or overhead (like rent or administrative expense) stayed the same, the cost per unit produced was bound to fall, even if the direct costs (wages, etc.) rose in line with output.

In practice, because of the learning curve, direct costs fell, too. It followed that the largest producer had the greatest economies of scale and thus the lowest costs and largest profits. That in turn enabled the volume leader to finance the investment in mechanisation that lowered costs still further.

In theory, then, biggest should always be best – and companies should continue to go for the largest possible volume and the largest possible plants. In fact, it doesn't work out that way any more – partly because labour problems tend to escalate as plants increase in size. Some companies now won't allow more than 200 or 500 employees on a single site.

Also, advances in production technology (as in CNC, FMS, robotics) have made it perfectly feasible to match the economies of very large, relatively inflexible plants on much smaller volumes. Developments of markets have moved in the same direction, as demand has become more segmented and the requirement for product variation more insistent.

But the economies of scale have not lost their power. They also exist in distribution (the more goods pushed through the same chain, the lower the unit cost will be), in purchasing power, and many other respects. Also, product line rationalisation can enable products in quite different market segments to participate in shared economies.

That partly explains the continued popularity of horizontal mergers. But the days are long past when a management could rest on its laurels – or its largeness. Merely observe how the Japanese car companies, by adopting the right product and production strategies, made mincemeat of the US motor mammoths – for all their economies of scale. (*See also*: Learning Curve; FMS/FMC; Product Line; Rationalisation; Horizontal Integration.)

EFFECTOR – Three meanings for the price of one word. First and simplest, whatever in a system operates it automatically – the sensor, for example, that shuts the whole system down on predetermined conditions. Second (still in the world of automation), effectors complete the cycle of cybernetics. To return to homeostasis, or the stable state, the effector, on receiving a note of a variance, alters the input to get the required change in output.

That, curiously enough, is what human effectors do as well. Those line managers are the people who implement and modify to make results come out according to plan. They are the agents for effective change – the essence of effectors, of course, being effectiveness. (*See also*: Cybernetics; Variance; Line.)

ELASTICITY – A price is elastic if you can raise it without reducing the sales volume of the article to which the price is attached to an unacceptable degree: for example (the worst example), to zero.

The price is inelastic if you can't put it up without knocking out sales. Even with an elastic price, though, you're likely to suffer a fall-off, either in total demand, or in the growth of that demand.

The vital question – how far can I raise the price without losing more than I gain? – can be answered precisely by an equation which establishes the degree of "price elasticity of demand": that is, the percentage change in demand that will follow a 1% rise in price (or a fall, for that matter; then the question is, How far can I cut the price without losing more [through lower margins] than I gain [through higher sales]?).

Understanding and use of this concept forms one of the indispensable business tools – underpricing being as great a threat to profits as overpricing. Many managements pillory themselves and fail to maximise profits by not doing their arithmetic. These show the CVG and CVL – the critical volume gain or critical volume loss. That means the amount by which sales must rise or fall to cancel out the benefits to profits of the price change. If sales forecasts indicate that you'll do better than the critical volume (i.e., make more money as a result of making the change), don't hesitate: make the move.

ELS – Economic lot size: the same meaning as EOQ. (*See also*: EOQ.)

EMV – Expected monetary value. Not to be confused with NPV or net present value. When you've worked out all the possible outcomes or payoffs of some action on which you've set your heart, you weight them according to your view of the probability of each payoff. The weighted arithmetic mean at which you then arrive is your EMV: only an idiot or an optimist, though, would expect this to be the actual outcome.

ENTREPRENEUR – Literally, from the French, someone who undertakes an enterprise – which in theory should mean every manager in business. Since the majority of managers, especially in bigger corporations, are about as enterprising as penguins, the word has become attached to the self-propelled, usually self-made businessman who starts up an enterprise or rejuvenates it – and because he owns the operation, wholly or in part, grows rich as it waxes.

The chief distinction between the entrepreneur and the manager is supposed to be that the latter doesn't take risks, while the former does. This doesn't mean that the entrepreneur's activities are riskier in the sense of being chancier – only that the entrepreneur is more prepared to take the chance of failure. Since failures are by no means uncommon in professionally managed companies, it follows that it isn't actually the risking of failure that distinguishes the entrepreneur; it's the attitude of mind, which, consciously or not, weighs the rewards of success against that risk.

Major corporations have wrestled for years with the problem of how to inculcate the entrepreneurial attitude of mind into their younger managers. The stumbling block is that, in most corporate structures, the managers neither own part of the business nor have the feeling, in any meaningful sense, that it is their own – to manage and develop to the best of their ability. But that's a failure not of the young executive but of the culture of the corporation.

ENTRY BARRIERS – An entry barrier exists where the price of competing in a new market is too high, because of the investment required, or where entry is made difficult to impossible by a physical stranglehold exerted by companies already in the market – for instance, because they possess patented or unique technology or control all the possible channels of distribution. As a generalisation, entry barriers have been growing lower and less important, partly because of the fluidity of new technology, partly because the capital-intensive industries (like steel) are ones that nobody wants to enter, partly because customer buying habits are changing so fast that openings for easy entry are constantly multiplying.

EOQ – Do you order the entire year's supply at one fell swoop? Or do you buy only as needed, at the very last minute? The first saves a deal of time and trouble, but lands you with heavy inventory costs. The second (unless you're in Japan) probably gives you a great deal more of both time and trouble – and higher purchasing costs.

The EOQ, or economic order quantity, is the answer: the amount which by combining the costs of carrying the stock and placing the orders gives you the lowest overall figure. You can find that blessed combination by trial and error, but it's a good deal easier to use this equation:

$$EOQ = \sqrt{\frac{2PY}{IU}}$$

where:

P = cost of placing an order (ordering costs)
Y = annual rate of demand (quantity)
I = stockholding cost as a decimal value of average stock value (storage costs)
U = unit cost

Better still, you can use *kanban* or just-in-time methods and get the best of both worlds. (*See also*: Kanban.)

EPOS – Electronic point of sale – the retailing end of the revolution in information systems technology (IST), and as much a revolutionary force as its equivalents in the factory or the office. The sci-fi dream of making the cash register an instrument of automatic stock control, automatic accounting, and automatic market research has come true – and nobody can yet tell how deep the results will run. (*See also*: IT.)

EPS – Earnings per share, the standard unit for stock market calculations, became a basic of management, too, because of the notion that the interests of management and those of the share-holders were united by the pursuit of a higher share price. EPS (obtained by dividing net profits by the number of ordinary shares outstanding) were the key, because the more they rose, the higher the share price would soar – other things being equal.

Hence, many US groups chose a given rate of annual rise in EPS (15% was a popular number) as the corporate target. All other targets were supposed to contribute to the achievement of this magic number, and gaps between targets and prospects were supposed to be plugged (mostly) by acquisitions. The EPS target was thus clearly linked with conglomeration and diversification.

But the disadvantages were – and are – deadly. First, share prices may or may not respond to rises in EPS. Second, the figure can be improved by devices (like those acquisitions) which may do little or nothing (or worse) for the health of the business. Third, EPS concentrates management minds excessively on the short term at a time when the Japanese have shown the vital importance of managing for the long term. Fourth, EPS tells you nothing about the basic strengths of the business in any of the areas – from effective production to market penetration – that really count.

In well-run companies today, EPS growth is only one of the numbers that top management seeks to enhance. It's still significant, though, because it measures the money from which the corporation can pay dividends. And that (although managements have tended to forget it) has always supposedly been the real name of the game.

EQUILIBRIUM PRICE – The price at which the demand for some product and its supply coincide. As a theoretical concept, this price of perfect balance must exist. In practical terms, if a price ever does reach equilibrium, it doesn't last long, and nobody knows that it's happened.

EQUITY – Has come to mean the same as shareholders' or investors' capital – though it's worth remembering that equity strictly refers to a specific right: the ownership of all the assets of the corporation after all other claims (i.e., those of the creditors, etc.) have been met. This ownership includes entitlement to all the profits remaining after debts have been settled and interest paid to banks and other lenders.

"All the profits" includes, of course, the retained profits. In the successful company the value of the equity should be constantly enhanced in real terms – that is, rising by more than the rate of inflation every year. Neither that nor continued real rises in dividends are part of the rights of the equity. They should be. (*See also*: Retained Earnings.)

ERG – Closely related to the hierarchy of needs, and coined by Clayton P. Alderfer. He reduced the Maslow hierarchy of seven classes of need to three – Existence, Relatedness, and Growth (hence, ERG). Existence means what it says: everything from food and drink to working conditions. Relatedness, too, is obvious: all relations with other people. Growth is the class of needs that push people onwards and upwards. The differences between Alderfer and Maslow are of more importance to the theorists than to people trying to manage people. (*See also*: Hierarchy of Needs.)

ERGONOMICS – Until relatively recent times, managements ignored the fact that workers and customers alike are affected by the physical environment in which they function – including the shape and dimensions of things like chairs and handles. To provide the mouthful definition (from the British Standards Institution) ergonomics is "The relation between man and his occupation, equipment and environment and, particularly, the application of anatomical, physiological and psychological knowledge to the problems arising therefrom".

In the factory and the office, major improvements in operator performance can be obtained by apparently minor alterations in the height of seating or other factors affecting the worker and his physical comfort in relation to his work. In the market, much backache has been spared by the amazing discovery by car and plane makers that some seats are more comfortable than others.

EXECUTIVE – The manager who works in and for the company is, by definition alone, an executive. Where the same man sits in another corporation's boardroom, he's non-executive, even though he can in theory (and should, in practice) have a real and sometimes decisive influence on how the executives execute.

Cases of non-executives conspicuously doing their duty by cracking down on the executives are much rarer than they should be – for several reasons. If the non-executive is an executive in another boardroom, he's not apt to encourage, by his own example elsewhere, the idea of his own non-executives throwing their weight around in *his* company. Then, the non-executives are really in the hands of the executive arm, which controls all the information flows and all the executive levers. Despite these drawbacks, non-executives have a big role to play – especially in fixing executive remuneration and making top appointments – the same function that in West Germany is filled by the *Aufsichtsrat*.

As for the executives, some are unquestionably more executive than others: line managers as opposed to staff. Hence the phrase "executive responsibility" – which means that some productive activity is going on, and that somebody is in charge and knows it, and so does everybody else. (*See also*: CEO; Aufsichtsrat; Line.)

EXIT BARRIERS – The opposite to entry barriers. The exit barrier exists where a corporation has very strong reasons (like heavy investment in fixed assets or a large market position built up over time) for refusing to leave a market, even though there are also powerful reasons for quitting – like low and declining profitability, or even a collapse in the market (as in the European car market in the late seventies and early eighties). It follows that entering an industry where the exit barriers are high is exceedingly risky – even though, from the established competitors' point of view, making an exit may well be the only sensible policy. (*See also*: Entry Barriers.)

EXPECTATION – In decision theory an expectation is the average result (usually a financial result) you should get if certain circumstances keep on coming around. In economics, "rational" expectations are those that anybody who is rational will form about the future. These expectations, however, will themselves affect the future.

For instance, if people believe, because of a drought in Ghana, that supplies of cocoa will be cut, and steep rises in price will follow, they will start to buy heavily – and events will come to pass exactly as they foresaw. The brilliant manager always bears in mind that markets are ultimately shaped by human motivation.

The trick (as difficult as it sounds) is to expect rationally how expectations themselves will force results to diverge from those that are expected. (*See also:* Decision Theory.)

EXPERT SYSTEMS – The first major practical application of artificial intelligence. The computer gets programmed to imitate the mind of a human who is expert in some particular field – like medical diagnosis, an expert application that is already well developed; but business managers aren't far behind the doctors in finding ways to exploit the combination of the computer's memory powers with the thought patterns of the expert human.

Examples of extant commercial systems include PROSPEC-TOR, which is used for geological searches, and is already said to have found one ore deposit that human investigators had overlooked; and FRUMP, employed by UPI in its news service for jobs that approximate the work of a human editor. Expert systems can perform such tasks by virtue of being fed with rules (for instance, "In such a situation, the chances are these . . ."). That's why they're quite good at games like backgammon and chess (for which 500 rules are needed – 50,000 if you want the system to beat a grandmaster).

What makes the system so expert is its ability to store the cumulative experience of many human beings, and to give an account explaining why it reached its conclusion. Already, these systems can, for instance, go behind the figures in a balance sheet to establish their true significance – and there's no doubt that the colossal fall in hardware costs, coupled with the increase in computing power, will see more and more expert systems reach the market. In fact, some human experts think that mimicry of human thought will replace the existing software approach altogether by the end of the century – and sooner rather than later.

Inexpert systems don't have the expert's full set of abilities, described by one writer as: "(1) performing operations with abstract entities, (2) accepting and passing on 'knowledge' from other systems, and (3) using knowledge correctly. These last three words are of paramount importance, since they imply some degree of understanding. The distinction between recognising and understanding can be described as the difference in language between grammar (what you can say) and semantics (what it means when you have said it). Finally, (4) expert systems have memory, although they are not generally able to learn by experience." The most important point, though, is that those systems are the ultimate in user-friendliness. You can talk to one like another human being – an exceptionally (and brilliantly) cooperative human, at that.

EXPONENTIAL SMOOTHING – In forecasting demand, and few things in management are more important, the basic objective, which is obvious, is to get it right; and the basic difficulty, which is equally obvious, is that it's impossible, except by luck. Knowing this, the expert forecaster notes the difference between past forecasts and actuals (what he calls the "actual observation").

The difference is the forecasting error, which he applies to his new forecast – only he doesn't apply all of the error, because some of it will have been random or chance. He therefore applies a "smoothing constant" of 0.1 or 0.2 to the error. The exponential bit comes in because, in the equation, earlier periods are given a greater weight than later ones.

This will be above the heads of non-mathematical managers. But the necessity for producing the most accurate possible demand forecasts had better not be beyond anybody. Everything from production schedules to the scale of the distribution network depends on the pattern of demand. While you've got to refer to the past as a basis and guide (which is where you need exponential smoothing, etc.), future demand obviously depends on a host of future factors on which educated estimates have to be made if uneducated errors are not to result.

EXTENSION – *See* Product Line.

F

FACILITIES – The most substantial form, generally speaking, of fixed assets: the plant and equipment and buildings that enable a company to conduct its business. Consequently, facilities planning is one of the most important activities in a corporation – though it's often one conducted with too little thought or forethought. Because of the finance-dominated way in which capital appraisal is carried out, usually going right up to board level, the question of investment in facilities tends to be determined by factors such as return on investment (or ROI).

What really matters, though, is what you're going to use the facilities for, and why. After all, it's no use investing in a facility that could double output at a healthy profit if the market for the product is actually going to halve – and don't think that hasn't happened. On the other hand, it's also no use failing to acquire new facilities because you don't like the ROI, only to find that as a result you're bound to lose market share as the market expands. And don't think that hasn't happened, either. (*See also*: Capital; ROCE/ROI.)

FACILITIES MANAGEMENT – Contracting out a specialist function (typically, a computer installation) to a specialist firm – lock, stock, and barrel. May not save money, but should save a deal of time and trouble – unless you've chosen the wrong specialist.

FACTOR OF PRODUCTION – Elaborate name for anything used in making anything – principally land, labour and capital, but not including the consumables eaten up in output.

FEATHERBEDDING – Highly expressive language to describe the employment of more people than necessary – usually many more – under pressure of strong unions. Notorious cases include Fleet Street before Wapping and the British public sector. Not to be confused with employment of excessive numbers by employers who aren't being blackmailed, but are just plain inefficient.

FEEDBACK – A relative newcomer to management terminology, gravitating from the world of computers to that of human beings with complete success. It now stands for any return flow of information to the manager – from the marketplace, from the employee (as in attitude surveys), and so on. Its technical meaning is the communication of the results of a system back to a comparator so that a variance or error can be detected and corrective action set going.

That's "negative" feedback. If you fail to act on the feedback, you may run into the dreaded "delay factor". In that case, the feedback becomes "positive" – and the system may, for example, churn out still more of an item that's already been overproduced because of the previous error.

The analogies with human feedback are obvious. If you don't act on the information coming from the work force or the marketplace, whatever's going wrong will get worse, perhaps with fatal effect. Effective management depends crucially on setting up systems to obtain excellent feedback, getting it, and then (above all) acting on the results. (*See also*: Attitude Survey.)

FEEDFORWARD – The errors which were fed back in the system and corrected during its operation are used for planning its future operations. There's no analogy yet between this aspect of automation and the conduct of businesses by human managers. Perhaps there should be. (*See also*: Feedback.)

FIFO/LIFO/NIFO – "First In, First Out" used to be the most popular way of accounting for stock consumption – many US companies still use it, though heaven knows why. The notion is that if you have two rarely used items in the warehouse, one bought in at £100 in 1975, the other at £200 in 1980, it's the first one you use first.

That maximises your profit (and your tax bill), but plainly grossly exaggerates the true situation. You've got to replace the item used, and that's going to cost at least £200. Hence "Last In, First Out". You charge the £200 item against the sales price – and thus protect the company from being taxed on profits made from holding stock: profits that aren't real, anyway, but which represent pure (or impure) inflation.

But wait: that item can't be bought for £200. It's going to be £250. What then? Since LIFO can't cope, you have to turn to NIFO – "Next In, First Out". If the tax man will allow NIFO, that ensures you are pricing your product high enough to cover your true costs. There's only one catch: NIFO methods may push the price up so high that you can't sell against the competition. In that case, you can forget about FIFO, LIFO, and NIFO, because no stock will be moving. If you're British, forget about LIFO and NIFO, anyway, for tax purposes: only FIFO is allowed.

FIRST-LINE MANAGEMENT – The supervisors are really the last line for management rather than the first – being the last stopping place for top-down instructions before (you hope) they are turned into reality by workers being supervised. But "first line" usefully conveys the fact that this is the place where everything happens – and where bottom-up management must begin.

The performance of first-line management used to be considered vital to overall results. It is still extremely important: but the advent of high technology, with its automated lines, and the development of methods for making the worker or a group of workers responsible for their own performance, has altered the role of supervisors – and diminished their numbers.

The changes have brought the first-line manager closer to the lines above. Now, he's likely to be an expert troubleshooter who fully understands the technology or tradecraft of the bit of the business that he's running. About time, too. (*See also*: Bottom-up.)

FMBG/FMCG – Fast-moving branded or consumer goods – as opposed to capital goods, other industrial products, and (presumably) slow-moving consumer goods. Mostly synonymous with packaged goods – the branded, own-brand (i.e., private label), or generic items that move in great quantity through supermarkets and like outlets. Because of their huge turnover and high volatility, FMCGs are the arena of maximum marketing horsepower and expenditure – and, of course, maximum joy in the ad agencies. (*See also*: Capital.)

FMS/FMC – Once upon a time, only engineers would have needed to know those letters and what they signify. That's all changed – the "flexible manufacturing system" is the key, not just to the "factory of the future", but increasingly to that of the present. FMS is the third stage in automation. It's what you get by linking NC (numerically controlled) machine tools and machining centres with robots and materials handling systems – plus a central computer to control the lot.

Why you want, rather need, to do something so complex is not merely to eliminate human labour costs (although that's a prime objective in the West and in Japan). It's because the demands of industrial and domestic consumers insist on increased variety and faster replacement of products. The problem for the manufacturer is to gain maximum flexibility, changing the output and input at will, without losing the economies obtained in the past by repetition.

This problem applies especially to the 70% or more of industrial output that hasn't been able to use the mass production systems first developed in Detroit. To quote Professor Gene Gregory of Sophia University in Tokyo, "Manufacturers found it increasingly necessary to build flexibility into their production systems so that they could supply more segmented markets with small lots of parts, components and finished products. Even more important, the growth of competition focussed attention on the fact that many manufactured products spend up to 95% of their time in the factory just waiting to be processed. New production systems were needed to obtain radical economies between stages."

Savings of skilled labour in small-batch production could be as great as 95% as FMS gets into its stride. But that's not where the future stops – even as it can be glimpsed now. Beyond the FMS lies the FMC – the flexible manufacturing complex. This needn't mean a whole factory. But it does mean that the five cells of the FMC will make parts, machine them, use lasers for cutting, welding, and treating, assemble the machined parts robotically, and inspect them automatically – all under the control of computers, and incorporating a CAD/CAM system. As to how the workers in the FMC will adapt to it, no need to worry: there will be hardly any. (*See also*: Automation; CAD/CAM.)

FOREMAN – The old name for front-line supervisor has gone out of fashion as the old function has changed. From being management's whip, the disciplinarian who got performance from the hands on the factory floor, the man in the front line now needs special skills, not just in the production process, but in the management of men and women. As methods of working in groups spread, his role becomes more that of leader than whip, the facilitator rather than the enforcer. In consequence, the selection and training of foremen or supervisors, or whatever you call them, should be in the forefront of the managerial mind – on the front line in that sense as well. (*See also*: Line; Group; Group Dynamics; Group Technology.)

FRINGE BENEFIT – Anything awarded to an employee beyond straight pay. The word fringe originally meant an extra, a present from a benign employer. But items like sick pay and pensions are now so widely available and expected that they are inseparable from other conditions of employment. The number and scope of what have consequently been restyled "employee benefits" will certainly expand as economic conditions allow.

The term "employee benefits" also has a public relations use, since fringe suggests (as in "fringe activity") something super-fluous and maybe not quite proper. Executives enjoying the fattest fringe benefit by far – the stock option scheme – naturally feel indignant about anybody thinking, even for a moment, that there's anything unnecessary, let alone improper, about their gains.

FUNCTIONAL – Marketing jelly beans is a function. Running the company that markets the jelly beans isn't. In earlier times, though, companies were mostly organised on functional lines: that is, the main functions (production, finance, marketing, per-sonnel, R&D) each had a director, and all subsidiaries had similar functional specialists reporting to him. These days, neither the strict separation of functions nor the diffusion of responsibility for success is thought healthy – functional organisation is definitely out.

The snag is that you still need the functions. In some cases (personnel, finance, R&D) the problem has been skirted. They have their own separate organisations within the organisation – and sometimes in the subsidiaries. For instance, a common approach to effective financial control is to have the finance man in the subsidiary report directly to the treasurer or finance director while ostensibly working for the subsidiary's boss.

This principle of matrix organisation has become particularly important as organisations have grown more complex, with more overlap between functions and more necessity to have many different kinds of cook preparing a given broth. What's vital, though, is that every function be given budgets and objects just as tight and demanding as any of the operating units. (*See also*: Matrix Organisation.)

FWH – Flexible working hours: the full title of what's better known as flextime or flexitime. Instead of reporting for fixed working hours every day, the employee has to be present only for a "core time" (usually in the middle period of the day, and lasting for, say, six hours).

The extra hours necessary under his or her conditions of work can be provided at any time the employee chooses – so, in effect, the employee, not the boss, elects when to start and finish work. Under the more advanced systems, deficits or surpluses of hours worked can be carried forward.

While usually and understandably popular with employees, FWH isn't easily applicable to many occupations (it's obviously best suited to office work) and introduces some administrative complexity. However, it does fit neatly into the now more libertarian ethos of work, and the future will surely be more flexible.

G

GAME THEORY – A lovely, esoteric, fun occupation for deep management thinkers. Any competitive market is like any game, in which (in its simplest, two-player form) any advantage for one must be a loss of equal size for the other (hence zero-sum game – one cancels out the other). In games (or markets) where there are more than two players, the problem is to choose the course of action which, when combined with all the other courses of action taken by all the other players, will yield you the highest number in the zero-sum outcome.

A subtle mathematical theory allows this choice to be made almost as an abstract exercise, provided that the following rules apply: (1) there's a specified set of possible choices, which all players know; (2) each player knows what outcome (i.e., result affecting all players) will result from every possible combination of choices; (3) everybody has ranked in order of preference the payoff (usually expressed in pounds) that he gets for his own side from each outcome; (4) each contestant knows the payoffs/preferences of all the others – and everybody must strive to get the highest one possible; (5) but (here's the catch) nobody knows what option anybody else has picked when making his own choice.

Well, such conditions may have existed at some time in the history of the planet – but not in most people's experience. Game theory is useful in making you put yourself in your competitor's shoes: but that should be instinctive anyway.

GANTT CHART – If you've ever drawn a graph charting tasks against the times when they must be begun and finished, and linking together associated tasks, you have followed in the footsteps of Henry Laurence Gantt. The principle can be applied to something as simple as writing a speech or as complex as building a nuclear power station.

The speech, for instance, will have to be delivered on a given day. Four interlinked stages are required: research, writing, typing, and rehearsal – and none of the last three can begin until the stage before is complete. Estimate the times, set them down in a graph form, and you have a timetable by which you can check actual performance. You can even use Gantt's standard set of symbols in a process which was the precursor of the computerised techniques, critical path method (CPM) and linear programming (LP), by which things like nuclear power stations actually are constructed.

Gantt was also the author of one of the many schemes for payment by results (PBR), with which the world has been afflicted. From a standard time per unit produced, Gantt worked out a standard output per week. That brought the standard, guaranteed minimum wage. Do better than that, and Gantt paid you 120% of the number of units you actually produced multiplied by the standard time per unit multiplied by the rate per hour. He called it the "task-and-bonus" system. At least the name is clear. (*See also*: CPM; Linear Programming; PBR.)

GCA – Group capacity assessment aims to solve the problem of making nonproductive departments productive – mostly in the clerical areas, but also in accounting and other backup operations. The GCA experts (like the Arthur Young accountancy practice, which developed the procedure) use work measurement techniques to decide how much work a department, or a group within a department, should be able to accomplish.

The standards thus decided are applied both to monitor how the departments actually perform and to provide more accurate figures for future staff needs. In clerical departments, as anywhere else, you get not what you pay for, but what you measure for.

GCF – Gross cash flow: what money the firm has left after paying out tax to the Inland Revenue, interest to its lenders, and dividends to the shareholders – plus the funds set aside for depreciation. Some think this is a better indicator of management's success in generating wealth than any of the more commonly used numbers – because it measures ploughback: the vital ingredient of survival and growth. (*See also*: Depreciation; Ploughback.)

GEARING – If ever there was a snare and a delusion, gearing is it. The term (translated into "leverage" by the Americans) refers to the effect on return on equity of financing the corporation by a heavier amount of debt. Take a million pound company (A) with 100 shareholders earning 20% on sales of £1 million, with no debt: that's £200,000, or £2,000 per shareholder for a £10,000 share – so far, so good.

But go further. Compare company A with an exactly similar company (B) with 10 shareholders financing 10% of the firm. The other 90% (£900,000) is debt, which gets interest of 10% –£90,000. The £200,000 profit is thus reduced to £110,000: but that's £11,000 for each £1,000 investor. The only catch, which explains why corporations don't aim for the maximum possible gearing, is that the whole marvel depends on the profits staying well above the interest payable. Suppose that company B's profits drop by half – to £100,000. Take away the interest payment, and the shareholders get only £1,000 each – no more than those in debt-free company A if its profits also halve.

If profits drop by three-quarters, though, company A's investors are still in the black, sharing £50,000. The As may not like that payment, but company B's people are far worse off. They're losing £4,000 apiece – for the interest still has to be paid.

The moral is that gearing is great if the business is great; if the business is great, though, you don't need to pay so much of the profits to the moneylenders. That's why prudent managements watch the debt-equity ratio with enormous care – that being the number which measures the level of gearing.

There's another form of gearing to which less attention is paid, though its impact can be very powerful; income gearing. This works to the advantage of large corporations. With £1 billion in shares and ROS of 5%, the corporation makes £50 million of trading profit. Cut the cost of sales (obviously, £950 million) by a mere 1%, and profits rise by £9.5 million (or 19%). The percentages work out in just the same way for a small company – but the numbers, alas, are nowhere near as large. (*See also*: Equity; Debt-Equity Ratio; ROS.)

GENERAL MANAGEMENT – It's less important to define general management than to get into it – and enter it you must if you want the most glittering prizes in business life. A manager whose job is defined by function (marketing, finance, personnel, production, etc.) is not in general management. A general manager probably has some functional people working for him – because the "general" in his title indicates a broad, cross-disciplinary responsibility for some part of the corporation.

The lines easily get blurred, though. For instance, the manager in charge of a plant, while his primary responsibility is for production, has a great deal of personnel work and a profound impact on the outcome of marketing and R&D efforts. For that reason, he may well be known as the "general manager" of the plant – even though, in many companies, that wouldn't admit him to the inner circle of general management: the policymakers and strategy kings back at head office.

The interconnections and overlaps inside a business are now so numerous and so strong that all managers with any real role in the corporate results (which should mean all managers) need to be generalists as well as specialists. Interestingly, this has long been a crucial element in Japanese practice. All executives are expected to be businessmen with a wide knowledge of functions other than their own. Thus any function, not just the amorphous area of "general management", can lead to the very top.

GIGO – Gunk in, gunk out. One of the first and truest acronyms of the computer age: it sounds as if it sprang from the disgruntled user rather than the alphabet-crazy computer specialist. The problem itself, that the quality of computer output depends on that of the input, ought not to worry anybody in these days of innumerable excellent programmes and innumerable number- and computer-wise managers. It probably still does worry people, though.

GO-GO – Describes managements whose go/no-go decisions are always go; it's thought the word comes from the French *à gogo* (as in "*whisky à gogo*"), meaning "galore" or "lots of". The "lots of" in a go-go outfit refers to lots of activity. The company seeks to attain super-growth by continuous bids and deals. This style of management, of funds and of companies, had its heyday in the sixties (which writer John Brooks styled as the "go-go years"). It's gone out of fashion since, for the good and sufficient reason that so many of the go-go people went broke.

GOING CONCERN – A basic assumption in corporate accountancy is that the business is going to continue trading – to go on. Its value is then normally higher than it would be if the company ceased trading, when its assets would have to be sold for what they would fetch – which might be less than book worth. Then all liabilities would have to be met, at once and in full, if possible. (*See also*: Book Value.)

GOLDEN – The adjective attached to any payment or financial arrangement that benefits an executive more than he deserves. The US "golden parachute" opens when the directors of a company (having previously provided themselves with their handy piece of air safety equipment) fail to prevent its acquisition. The parachute then opens, showering the executives with financial compensation that may be so generous that (knowing about it in advance) the predator is put off his feed.

The "golden handshake" rewards a failed individual as opposed to a failed board. To compensate for his dismissal, the executive is paid off with a lump sum (the gold) and a limp right grip (the handshake). Such payments used to be entirely tax free, meaning that it was more lucrative to be fired than to work. Despite some tightening up of the tax rules, it still is.

GO/NO GO – The crucial point in decision making, where management must decide to proceed with a project or drop it. It concentrates everyone's mind wonderfully to have a firm date by which the go/no go decision must be taken – otherwise things can just drift on pointlessly for far too long.

GOODWILL – Every business has goodwill – but you can only find out what it's worth by selling the organisation. It's the prime asset among the intangibles: what the company is worth above and beyond the amount that you might expect from the money numbers. On a sale, the goodwill not only surfaces in the transaction itself, but may also survive on the balance sheet of the purchaser.

It's normally calculated as the difference between the book value of the assets acquired and the price paid for the company. Since nobody likes to believe that he's paying good money for nothing (though experience shows that he often is), the difference has to be the goodwill that the buyer believes the purchased company possesses. (*See also*: Intangibles; Book Value.)

GOZINTO CHART – This shows the route, vital in production engineering, by which manufactured parts get formed into sub-assemblies and sub-assemblies into complete assemblies. It shows, simply, what "goes into" what.

GRIEVANCE – One of the best ways of getting bad labour relations is to mishandle complaints by employees – whether justified or not. Long experience in well-managed companies proves that the best results follow from a very carefully organised hierarchy of stages in dealing with grievances, so that the aggrieved employee, if still dissatisfied after any stage, can take his grievance to the next stage in the hierarchy – ultimately, to the summit of the company.

The guarantee cuts two ways, demonstrating to the employee that he or she will get justice, but also assuring top management that employee abuses won't be bottled up lower down. It helps further to establish a channel for anonymous grievances – IBM calls them "speak-outs". These speak-outs will often be frivolous, just as grievances will often be unjustified. But because grievances are always justified in the eyes of the aggrieved, and because the company with no real grievances would not only be wonderful, but not of this world – because of these truths, a proper grievance policy is essential to effective management of people.

GROSS – Referring to the income of a corporation, gross means before taxation – but is rarely used, pretax profit being preferred. That presumably is to avoid confusion with gross margin, or gross profit, which is most commonly used by retailers to mean the price received for the goods sold, less the cost of buying same. Obviously, the shop will have overheads and other selling costs to take into account before arriving at the true profit. But all competent shopkeepers have an exact idea of what gross they need in order to end up at the end of the day with plenty of cash in the till.

GROUP – Once used mostly in its legal or financial function (meaning companies under common ownership), group has come into its full glory with the rise of human relations theory. The sociologist's work group (that is, people working on a common task, usually in a plant) has linked hands with the psychologist's interactive group (that is, any get-together of individuals for some purpose) to form a whole new strategy of man-management and plant organisation.

At one extreme, group decision, the manager abdicates the role of solving problems himself. Instead his job is to lay the problem clearly before the members of the group, and to let them decide. The manager's aim is simply to get the optimum decision. He may even have been given training in group dynamics (the study of how people behave in groups, in particular their relationship with other members and the group as a whole).

The use of these techniques is comparatively rare, but the philosophy of group organisation is becoming universal – that the basic unit in a plant or office is the group (the equivalent of the family in society at large) and that the best performance and highest motivation will be achieved by reaching the individual through the group. Hence group incentive payments that reward the worker, not for his own endeavours, but for those of the group. Which means he'd better not let them down. Or they him.

GROUP DYNAMICS – The study of people in groups. Management is essentially a group activity – so modern seekers after management success have been paying more and more attention to man the member as opposed to man the individual. Antony Jay, in *The Corporate Man*, has even put forward the notion that there's a natural primordial size of hunting group (no larger than a football team, say) beyond which success gets much harder – if not impossible – to achieve.

Be that as it may, group dynamics has given birth to group dynamics training (also known as "laboratory training"), in which the results of the study are used with the object of improving group performance. The T-group form of sensitivity training is one such method. People in group training can be "cousins" (same firm, same level, but not normally working with each other); "family" (they do work together); or "strangers" (no connection).

Beyond training, the deliberate use of groups in real life includes grouping machines and men together so that the group produces an entire assembly or sub-assembly; providing incentives on a group rather than an individual basis, even advancing to group decision, as propounded by the US psychologist Norman Maier. (*See also*: T-Group; Incentive.)

GROUP TECHNOLOGY – A revolutionary approach to batch production. You group together those bits and pieces that are processed on similar equipment using similar processes. This speeds up output and reduces waiting between stages. Also, it's a better background for introducing group incentives and like ways of mobilising worker cooperation. No doubt, because it *is* both radical and effective, GT has been adopted only slowly – it is now, in any case, being overtaken by the latest developments in automation. (*See also*: Batch Production; Automation.)

GROWTH COMPANY – A strange term: one of the strangest in the lexicon of corporate praise, but also one of the vaguest and most evanescent. It means a company that is dedicated to fast growth, that has proved it by growing fast, and that is confidently expected to go on growing in the future.

What kind of growth isn't specified – whether in sales, profits, assets, or earnings per share. Even if a company does grow fast on all four counts, it's unlikely to retain growth-company status unless the share price is also growing fast. But how fast is fast? Again, there's no specific answer – and companies that do commit themselves to a hard number (like 15% per annum) often find that it's very hard indeed.

Those that fail on such hurdles are said to have gone "ex-growth" – even though their vital statistics may still be expanding. The truth of the matter is that organic growth has to be the objective of all companies that don't want to go backwards, that "growth company" and "growth stock" are just fashionable labels. Curious fact: there's no antonym, no opposite, for a growth company – one indicator that maybe growth company doesn't mean much itself. (*See also*: Organic Growth.)

H

HALO EFFECT – A phenomenon in marketing research and in performance appraisal. People will say they buy a prestigious product when they don't; people will rate a person as strong because he has come across as decisive in one situation. In appraisal, the halo effect works the other way – give a dog a bad name, and a bad reputation will stick to him. In which case the alternative wording to halo effect is better: horns effect.

HARVESTING – A company engages in a harvesting strategy when it deliberately allows its market share to decline. The reason is to maximise cash flow and short-term earnings from the business concerned – short-term being the operative word, since there's obviously no interest in (and little possibility of) a long-term future. The process has similarities to that covered by another agricultural metaphor: milking a "cash cow". The difference is that harvesting is usually a policy enforced by dire need, like a cash shortfall, while the cash-cow approach is a strategic choice. Both may, however, end up in the same place: with the company out of the business altogether. (*See also*: Cash Cow.)

HAWTHORNE EFFECT – Productivity responds to environmental change – any change – that is presented to the work force as a means of raising productivity. That's the Hawthorne effect in a nutshell. There can't be many experiments, in any field, conducted as long as half a century ago that are still referred to so often and with such respect as those done in a factory near Chicago owned by Western Electric. From 1927 to 1932, the 29,000 workers making telephones at the Hawthorne plant were subjected to observations that nobody has yet contradicted.

The original idea was only to investigate the effect of different levels of lighting on worker performance. But the investigations were extended to other working conditions – like working hours, when rest breaks were taken, and types of incentive payments. The results all led to the same conclusion – that it wasn't so much what management did, but the fact of its taking an interest in working conditions, and changing them, that produced improvements in productivity.

For exactly the same reasons, the gains were not permanent. The Hawthorne effect constantly needs topping up if the productive momentum isn't to be lost. This knowledge has two important applications. First, always treat the results of changes in raising productivity with caution – *allowing for the Hawthorne effect*. Second, constantly renew the effect by finding new ways of stimulating the workers' juices.

HEAD OFFICE – Corporate headquarters, the centre of the company, where the ultimate power and control, the keys of the money box and the highest-paid managers customarily reside. The fashion is for head office to be scaled down from the 1,000-plus of a company like ITT in its prime.

Many companies with sales in the billions now make do with 300 or so corporate people – some with far less. You shouldn't *need* many if the company is divided into the segmented, market-oriented units, run by general managers with the authority they require, which is the modern trend (and quite right, too).

HEDGING – A sport of very little significance before the days of floating exchange rates and the advent of futures markets in practically anything. Whatever may be done with money involves a risk, even if you keep it in your own currency: another currency may rise against it. Even the wisest man doesn't always make the wisest decision – so he takes out insurance.

If he's got some yen coming his way in three months' time, he sells that amount of yen now, at today's price for delivery then. If the Japanese currency collapses in the interim, he's covered against the loss. Such deals are now everyday practice for international companies, which could otherwise lose fortunes if a major currency moved against them.

The same principle applies to commodities, another volatile number. The company that's buying cocoa or copper for its future needs is foolish in the extreme if it doesn't protect itself against the possibility of a price slump – or surge. You can even use the hedging principle for two-way bets. For instance, a financier who fears that the election of a Labour Government will force down his shares places a large bet on the nose of the very party he loathes and fears. If Labour wins, he collects: if it loses, he still collects.

HERZBERG – Frederick Herzberg is the American psychologist whose work on "job satisfaction" has probably been most influential. He separated out the "motivators" from the "hygiene factors". The latter aren't directly concerned with the job's content, though they may certainly seem to be – things like working conditions, pay, relationships with other workers and with your bosses. Get these things right, and you won't have a dissatisfied worker – but you won't necessarily have a satisfied one, either.

To achieve that Holy Grail of motivation, you've got to concentrate on the job content: what the task actually consists of (is it boringly repetitive or creative and varied?); what hopes of getting promotion go with the job; how much satisfaction, recognition, and reward the worker gets from doing it well. Herzberg holds that these factors work the other way around from hygiene elements. Get them right, and you've got a satisfied worker. So far, so good. But get them wrong, and he's unlikely to be dissatisfied. At least, that's the theory. (*See also*: Job Enrichment.)

HEURISTICS – Another way of saying trial and error. When you can't solve a problem by any other means, heuristics (from the Greek for discovery) is the only course available. In the hands of the management scientist, though, trial and error isn't hit or miss. The computer makes possible a simulation of the problem and a rapid run through the alternatives to find the best. (*See also*: Simulation.)

HIERARCHY – The classic form of business organisation has a base of first-line supervisors, each reporting to a single boss in the next layer, each of whom reports to a single boss in the next layer ... and so on, until the ultimate boss (the boss of bosses) is reached at the apex of the pyramid.

Salary scales accord with the steps, rising at carefully calculated intervals, all of which can be mapped out prettily on an organisation chart. It sounds like a bureaucracy – and that's what it is – which explains why hierarchical modes are increasingly being broken. The organisation pyramid is neat and tidy, and everyone knows his or her place. But is that what you want in a fast-changing world where flexibility is worth more than hierarchy? The answer's obvious: no. (*See also*: Line; First-line Management.)

HIERARCHY OF NEEDS – Abraham H. Maslow coined the phrase to define his own theory – that man progresses from need to need in a series of five hierarchical steps. The five are: (1) physiological needs, e.g., for food to alleviate hunger, for drink to remove thirst, for clothing to protect from the weather, etc.; (2) safety and security needs: protection from loss or danger; (3) belonging and love needs: the sense of being part of a group; (4) recognition needs: the need to feel respected by others; (5) the need for self-actualisation, namely the need to feel that one has achieved personal fulfilment.

You can use the concept in two main ways: in marketing and in man management. In the first usage, the marketer looks to see which needs, at which psychological level, his product or service is satisfying. The more needs it satisfies, the higher the perceived value of the offering will be – and the higher the price that can be charged for it.

A classic example is the revived and refurbished Orient Express train. All it does is meet a basic need for transport, which it does neither efficiently (it's slow) nor economically (it's expensive). But travelling on the train plainly appeals to needs in hierarchic levels – Three and Four (above) – maybe even Five.

In man management, the argument is that basic needs must be satisfied first, before the higher-order needs can be effective as motivators. That being done, though, the more a job satisfies needs above the first two primary levels, the more motivated the employee will be, and the more effectively he or she will work. Whether or not that's true, it's become increasingly important to structure jobs and organisations so that they do allow progression through the whole gamut of Maslow's hierarchy.

HISTORICAL – Accounting used to concern itself solely with history – what's happened already – and public company accounts are still historical, adding up the figures for events that took place, in some cases, over a year before, and valuing items not at their present-day worth but on the basis of amounts paid in the past, sometimes in the distant past.

Nowadays managers are more interested in the present and the future, which is why the emphasis in budgeting has shifted from the historical (how the last quarter compared with the same period a year before) to the immediate and the impending (how the last quarter's results compared with forecast, why any discrepancies arose) – and, most important, to what all this signifies for the quarters ahead.

The technique called "historical costing" is still used for things like special orders, where standard costing can't be applied. The records are used to find out exactly how much the things actually did cost, complete with absorption of overheads. The results are then compared with the estimates on which the price was based. Sometimes they even agree. (*See also*: Budget; Standard; Absorption.)

HORIZONTAL INTEGRATION – When you group together businesses of like nature, the integration is called horizontal; and the point of the deal is to get economies of scale in manufacturing, marketing, and distribution, cutting out duplication and maximising the impact per pound in spending in vital areas such as R&D.

The classic horizontal merger was the making of General Motors – though the development of that colossus over time demonstrates that mergers of this type can seldom get very far without also indulging in integration of the opposed kind: the vertical variety. (*See also*: Vertical Integration.)

HORIZONTAL PRODUCT/MARKET SELECTION – In choosing the products and markets in which to compete, a company that selects those where it already has a position (that is, it sells the new products to the same end-users) is making a horizontal choice. The horizontal company looks to its existing strengths, in technology, reputation, etc., and plans to build on these in order to obtain a competitive advantage. By the same token, it also tries to avoid areas where the corporate weaknesses will impose a serious disadvantage: unless, that is, the company's management is not thinking clearly – as often happens.

HORNS EFFECT – *See* Halo Effect.

HOT MONEY – Could be hot in the criminal sense (e.g., Mafia money), in which case it is moved from country to country to avoid detection. Or, could be moved from country to country not to escape detection but simply to grab the highest going rate of interest in the world.

HUMAN ENGINEERING – Sounds alarmingly like what went on in Dr Frankenstein's lab, but is only a name for ergonomics, and also for human factors engineering, which has the disadvantage of being one word longer. (*See also*: Ergonomics.)

HUMAN RELATIONS SCHOOL – First F. W. Taylor begat Taylorism, or scientific management. Next, Henri Fayol begat administrative management, aided and abetted by Mary Parker Follett, Luther Halsey Gulick, Lyndall F. Urwick, *et al*. Then the Hawthorne experiments begat the human relations school, which rules the roost to this very day.

The various contributors to this school of thought all stress the need to develop individual potential by successful relations with others in the group. Greatly in tune with the spirit of a democratic, egalitarian, sociologically conscious age, the human relations school has contributed much to the evolution of ideas on participation in management – though actually it's a gross libel on Taylor, the first begetter, to say that he ignored human relations. Like any sensible manager, he valued and stressed them enormously. (*See also*: Taylorism; Hawthorne Effect; Group; Participation.)

HUMAN RESOURCES ACCOUNTING – "People are our most important asset." So companies have often boasted, truly enough, but not to any great effect – since the people concerned seldom receive the treatment owed to this importance. Human resources accounting sought to redress the balance – literally. The value of the labour force, and the sums invested in its training and development, would be entered in the balance sheet, just like the sums deployed in plant and machinery. A gimmick, and a silly one.

HURDLE RATE – Woe betide the investment project which – in a firm that has such a thing – can't get over the hurdle rate. That's the minimum IRR (internal rate of return) which the top management will allow. It's a distinctly unskilful manager, though, who can't cook the figures sufficiently well to get over the hurdle. Whether the actual project will do so when completed is quite another matter. (*See also*: IRR.)

HYGIENIC MANAGEMENT – If wages are high, employee benefits generous, working conditions good, and management attentive to the work force – then, by the criteria of Frederick Herzberg, the management is hygienic. In other people's eyes, the management is just practising good old-fashioned paternalism. The difference is that the paternalists, the latter-day descendants of Victorians who took a cradle-to-grave interest in their work-people, expected the grateful employees to work harder. The Herzberg school regards the hygiene factors only as preconditions for the true motivators from which harder and better work really springs. (*See also*: Herzberg.)

HYPE – Hyping used to have the connotation, not just of ultra-heavy promotion, but of unjustified claims. The claims may still be false, but the word has come to mean the orchestrated promotion (typically, of a book, or movie personality), in which every available publicity technique is used to create demand and/or the appearance of demand for whatever or whoever is being hyped. The word may come from "hyperbole", meaning extravagant, exaggeration, or just from "hyper", the prefix meaning very, very. Whatever the etymology of the hype, you know when it's happening – if some movie actor suddenly appears on every chat show in town his and the hypers' motives are nothing but ulterior.

I

INCENTIVE -- All work rests on incentive, but not all work recognises the fact. Argument has raged for decades over whether men and women work better if the results of their labour are converted directly into more money for themselves. At the upper end of the scale, among senior executives in the United States, the argument has long gone by default. Almost everybody gets a results-linked bonus, sometimes of stupefying size.

Argument continues, though, over a different matter – whether there's any effective link between the performance and the results, and whether the usual criteria (short-term profits) take the eyes of the executives off the far more important matter of long-term maximisation of the business. In other words, it's doubtful that these executive programmes work as incentives, and uncertain whether the incentive used is the right one, anyway.

At the lower end of the scale, despite such schemes as those of Rucker and Scanlon, incentive pay is much less widespread. It was once almost universal in any manufacturing industry, where work would be measured by the piece – hence "piecework". The more pieces a person produced, the more he or she got paid: with the same rate for every piece.

Among several weaknesses, piecework had the great defect that it made no allowance for mechanisation. If faster machines doubled output, why should the operator get doubled pay? For this and other reasons, PBR (payment by results) schemes are now far more complex – including the variety based on added value. Their very complexity helps explain their restricted popularity. A pity, since they can work wonders. (*See also*: Rucker Plan; Scanlon Plan; PBR; Added Value; Piecework.)

INCREMENTAL – An incremental cost is what you get by increasing output, say, as opposed to the cost you incur by staying put. An incremental price is a polite word for what at the extreme gets damned as dumping. The firm covers the full costs (direct and indirect, variable and fixed) on, say, the output destined for the domestic market. It then prices the export production to cover only the variable costs (and also make a profit, it hopes).

There are limits to how far the practice can go. If the price differential is too great, it opens the door to profitable arbitrage – with domestic opportunists buying abroad and shipping back to undercut the supplier on the home market. That happened when it became cheaper to buy British cars in Belgium and ship them back to the UK – much to the disgust of the car companies. (*See also*: Arbitrage; Dumping.)

INDUSTRIAL DEMOCRACY – A more pointed and idealistic phrase for employee participation – but misleading because of its idealism. While the worker can be given a voice in the running of the business, he can't in most circumstances be given a vote – which is the essence of true democracy. So the industrial variety comes to mean the provision of representative institutions through which worker views can be expressed to management.

In some cases, where ownership control has been handed over to the workers completely, the appearance of democracy comes closer to reality. Employees may even have the ultimate sanction of removing the boss – but, until they do, either he manages in the undemocratic way of most bosses or the company is mismanaged – which does nobody any good. (*See also*: Participation.)

INDUSTRIAL ENGINEERING – The activity at which Americans used to be supreme – they invented the concept. While it takes in lesser (but still essential) disciplines like work study, industrial engineering goes beyond that to embrace the whole activity of the plant.

The key phrase here is "total system", reflecting the unavoidable fact that everything inside the plant interrelates with everything else, and that resources won't be used to their optimum unless the interrelationships are balanced and integrated. If the concept had been pursued more vigorously (and rigorously) in the sixties and seventies, the Japanese wouldn't have been able to make the sharp gains in manufacturing costs which, in the eighties, US manufacturers are striving to reverse – by better industrial engineering, of course. (*See also*: Work Study.)

INDUSTRIAL MARKETING – The opposite, or rather the poor relation, of consumer marketing (*see* FMCG). The industrial marketer sells exclusively to other companies, and therefore needs different techniques and research methods. The game lacks the glamour of consumer-marketing, but it's the bedrock of business – and the sharp end of profit generation for most manufacturing corporations.

INERTIA SELLING – It seems a great idea to send a person some goods unasked – and to treat it as a sale unless he returns the article within a set period. The inertia comes in because a large number of involuntary buyers won't return the goods, through simple inertia – and then they get dunned for payment.

One of the earliest developments in consumerism was the conviction that people should be protected against their own weaknesses, including their inertia. This selling practice – a pretty shabby one, at that – has been outlawed in many places. However, the techniques of direct response advertisers include a fair amount of more discreet use of inertia – sometimes even an unfair amount. (*See also*: Consumerism; Direct Response.)

INFLATION ACCOUNTING – As was predicted (by the author), hyper-inflation has been and gone before the accountants have agreed on how to account for it – making any future agreement which they happen to achieve academic unless the inflationary engine starts up again.

The purpose of inflation accounting is to remove the effects of inflation from the balance sheet and hence from the profit-and-loss account. The latter is most easily done by restating the surplus of revenues over cost in constant money. But that rough and ready method doesn't take into account the fact that the company makes some gains from inflation – for instance, its debts are worth less when repaid than they were when incurred.

Add to this the complexities of accounting for stock and for the replacement of plant and machinery, and you arrive at a figure which, while it doesn't overstate the profits (which historic cost accounting does to an alarming degree during hyper-inflation), is even more of an abstraction from reality than present corporate accounting. And that's saying a lot. (*See also*: CCA.)

IN-HOUSE – One of the unending debates in any company is whether to conduct certain of its activities inside the company or out. Training is one of the controversial areas; so is product design; so is component supply; so is labour-only subcontracting – in fact, the number of areas where companies can choose between in and out is now so great that you could in theory reduce the corporation to little more than a handful of executives and a board – and, maybe, conduct its business at lower cost by doing everything practical out-of-house.

That's the nub of the issue: whether, assuming that the company has the capability to provide the service in-house, or can acquire that capability, the cost, for a given satisfactory level of service, will be less inside than out. In some circumstances, it may be worth incurring extra cost for other reasons – like commercial secrecy. But in a large number of cases, companies are (or would be) better off for taking the inside outside. (*See also*: Labour-only.)

INNOVATION – The introduction of anything new to the market served by the company – or, in some circumstances, to the company itself. The apparent paradox is explained by the fact that innovation is customarily associated only with product development – though in fact highly profitable innovations can be produced in internal systems of which the ultimate customer is never aware – and which the competition may never emulate.

While this form of innovation (doing internal things better/
differently) has received little attention, concern with product and
process innovation has become almost overwhelming in the West
as the need to raise productivity and to win competitive advantage
has become uppermost in managers' minds. For many companies, however, innovation is still identified with R&D –
although in fact the activities are associated but different.

It's the innovator who brings the original idea to R&D, or who
finds a way of exploiting the work coming from the labs. In
recognition of this, companies are now making innovation a major
distinct activity, usually under a title such as "New Product
Department" – while also setting up procedures to ensure that all
ideas are well and truly screened.

The evidence is clear that companies which are wide open to
new product or service suggestions from any source, but rigorous
in the examination and execution of these ideas that seem worthy
of further expenditure, do far better than companies that narrow
the channels for innovation ideas, but are less organised in their
follow-up. And the pundits are quite right; failure in innovation
really is a recipe for failure all-round. (*See also*: R&D.)

INSIDER – Any director or employee of a company is by definition
an insider who possesses inside information about a corporation.
That's fine, so long as the insider doesn't act on what he knows, by
buying or selling the shares – or getting his nearest and dearest to
do so. If he does, the wrath of the authorities will descend on his
head. That, you may think, has killed insider trading stone dead.
Would it were true.

INTANGIBLES – Assets that don't exist in any physical sense now
account for an increasing and sometimes overwhelming proportion of a company's assets. Extreme examples are advertising
agencies and similar service businesses, like consultancies, that
have no physical assets to speak of, but whose value resides in the
intangible asset of the quality of their personnel and the work
these people do.

For accountancy purposes, rightly, intangibles are seldom

given any value on the balance sheet – even though some (like trademarks) could be sold for much money. The strict approach is also usually applied to R&D, although, in a high-tech company, the cumulative R&D outlay, and the patents developed by that expenditure, will be the most valuable and possibly the most expensive assets on the premises.

When intangibles do exist on the balance sheet, it's usually in the form of goodwill. The persistence of intangibles on the balance sheet, though, isn't a good sign. The sooner the intangible goes, the more tangible the will of the management. (*See also*: Goodwill.)

INTER-FIRM COMPARISON – Your business may look wonderful to you – but it may not look as good to a competitor, and it may actually not be as good by his standards. Mainly by the use of ratios, companies in similar industries and circumstances can compare performance against each other. If they all strive to raise performance on every count to the highest in the bunch, magical monetary results should flow – although a basic law of management lays down that, however good you get, you can always get better. (*See also*: Ratio.)

INTERPERSONAL – How people relate to each other, in and out of groups, has become a major preoccupation of management thinkers since the human relations school came into the ascendant. The identification of relations among persons as the key to many management concerns may not have made it any easier to solve problems – but it has at least focused attention on the fact that they exist. (*See also*: Human Relations School.)

INVENTORY – The stock of goods that a company maintains – its materials, finished goods, supplies, work-in-progress. Being a prime area for fraud, this is where the accountants fasten their beadiest eyes. So should managers; not just to ensure that "shrinkage" (i.e., loss or plain theft) is within acceptable bounds, but to check one of the basic factors in profitability – stock-turn, or the value of annual sales divided by the value of inventory.

If it's easier to do the sum the other way round (that is, if the inventory is worth more than the annual sales) the business is almost certainly being managed atrociously – and is losing money on the extra capital tied up in excessive inventory. If the ratio hasn't come down over the last few years, that's another bad sign, for automated warehousing and methods like *kanban* have greatly reduced the amount of stuff you need to keep around the premises. If a change in production method and layouts doesn't also improve stock-turn, you're doing something wrong. (*See also*: Kanban, WIP.)

INVESTMENT – A present sacrifice for a potential future gain. The principal distinction between capital and current in company accounts is that cash generated from the current account is invested and then becomes capital (adding to the capital worth of the firm). That's pure bookkeeping, but the addition to the value is pure fact – the firm that underinvests loses worth just as surely as the firm that invests badly and loses all the money invested.

Investment takes several different forms. In any company, a large part of the capital spending has to be on replacement of plant and equipment that is worn out or obsolete, i.e., can no longer perform its task at an economic cost or is committed to a technology that has been overtaken.

Replacement merges into the second category, expansion, because of the strong possibility that the new equipment will not be exactly the same as that being replaced, and that its extra qualities will include the ability to produce more. Expansion may not, of course, be in lines already produced – in which case the investment is in innovation (even if somebody else is producing the product or service, it's an innovation for the business embarking on it for the first time).

At this point, the lines between capital and current get blurred. Is spending on R&D that results in an innovation an investment expenditure or not? Since current cash is being sacrificed for future gain, the answer should be that it's an investment. But conventional accounting and conventional wisdom alike hold that you should write off all R&D as current spending – because of uncertainty over whether a saleable asset will in fact result from the outlay.

For the same reason, it's thought wrong (and it is) to treat expenditure on a product launch as investment – even though the money invested in making the product can't be recovered without the marketing money. But these accountancy arguments are beside the main point, which is that if a company or a country invests too little (as British industry did from after the war onwards) the result will be a serious loss of competitive power. (*See also*: Capital; Current; R&D.)

INVESTMENT APPRAISAL – The habit of treating capital expenditure as the key to boardroom control of corporations made it imperative to develop better – or apparently better – methods of assessing projects for spending capital. Actually, nobody has been able to agree on which is the best out of a package that includes discounted cash flow (DCF), net present value (NPV), internal rate of return (IRR), or even good old-fashioned payback. All are only different ways of looking at the same picture – a picture painted by the amount of money sunk into the project before the inward flow of money from sales starts to exceed the outward flow of costs, and by the relation of that positive cash flow to the sunk amount. Since appraisal rests on forecasts of capital costs that can undershoot by as much as 1,000% (as for some nuclear plants) and on projections of earnings that are sometimes even worse, you can see that the detailed, pinpoint accuracy of appraisal exercises, while unavoidable, is spurious. (*See also*: Capital; DCF; NPV; IRR; Payback; Cash Flow.)

IRR – The internal rate of return is attached to the concept of net present value. NPV gives you the figure for today's total value of the project, valued over as many years ahead as you like, with the actual cash flows devalued by whatever interest rate you've chosen. The IRR is the further annual percentage needed to reduce the NPV to zero. This percentage gives you what's sometimes called the "yield", the "yield rate", or the "earning power" of the investment – and it had better have plenty of the last. (*See also*: Yield.)

IT – Information technology – another name for EDP (electronic data processing). As the range of computer-aided services has widened, especially since the advent of the computer-on-a-chip, or microprocessor, so EDP has come to seem inadequate to describe all the wonders made manifest. True, IT does embrace word-processing and telecommunications, videotext and microfiche, filing and databases, microcomputers and mainframes, in a more satisfactory manner than EDP, though so wide a definition is too wide to have much meaning.

J

JABMAS – The Japanese business and management system. The JABMAS acronym is mostly used by those who, to use the words of one critical study, are touting the system "as the panacea for all that currently ails business firms in the United States, Canada and West Europe". Of course, the critics are right: JABMAS is no panacea, not even a sovereign remedy; and ABMAS (the American business and management system) has a lot going for it. But ABMAS still has a lot to learn from JABMAS – which, after all, has taken much of its substance and much of its strength from the former.

JOB DESCRIPTION – A great favourite of personnel bureaucrats, the job description specifies exactly what the job-holder is supposed to do, delineates his responsibilities, lays down his reporting and other relationships. Lack of job descriptions can result in sloppy, confused management. Excessive reliance on them results in constipated, inflexible, and ultimately unrealistic management – and in badly done jobs.

JOB ENRICHMENT – Once upon a time, the only connection between jobs and enrichment was the money handed over. When the money motivation seemed to be losing its force, the sociologists, then in full vogue, had a convincing explanation. Man needed more than money – he needed job satisfaction, and that could only be achieved by making the job itself more attractive, by "enriching" it.

That meant giving the worker more responsibility, allowing him more say over how the job was done, giving him extra tasks. If you want to know the difference between this and "job enlargement", there isn't much: the job of any assembly-line worker is enlarged by giving him more to do than the one repetitive task that was all that the traditional organisation of work allowed in mass production.

Events have overtaken the sociologists, though. The advent of advanced automation, with its flexible manufacturing systems (FMS) and robotics, has changed the nature of factory work. In any case, the theory of effective organisation of work has moved away from the assembly line to the group: away from single-task repetition to giving the group and the worker responsibility for a whole assembly. The job thus gets enriched automatically: whether the individual does, too, is quite another matter. (*See also*: FMS/FMC; Group; Robotics.)

JOB EVALUATION – The cynics would say that you can always tell a bureaucracy from an entrepreneurial outfit by its job descriptions. The only reason why you need to describe or rank (evaluate) a job is to establish its position in a pecking order and (far more meaningful to one and all) a pay scale.

To be fair, though, you don't have to be bureaucratic, merely big, to need tools like the "factor comparison method", "job grading", or "points rating". The mistake is to imagine that these necessary administrative procedures in the cause of organisational tidiness are anything more than the barest bones of a business.

JOINT CONSULTATION – A stage on the long march towards full co-determination, though joint consultation is well established in many companies whose managements haven't the faintest intention of sharing any power. The joint consultation machinery provides for meetings with employee representatives at which management may announce any plans that will affect employees' futures, but at which the main subjects tossed about are all those currently on employees' minds except pay and conditions – which are reserved for collective bargaining between the employer and the unions. A definite advance on the mushroom school of management, which holds that companies grow best if everyone's kept in the dark. (*See also*: Co-determination; Collective Bargaining.)

JUNIOR BOARD – Some companies set up committees below top management, but which behave just like a full board of directors. That is, they consider the company's performance, review its plans, recommend policies to the top management – and, no doubt, nobody takes any notice of them. To be sure, that's sometimes true of real boards . . . The junior groups are a feature of "multiple management", the method of employee participation thought up by Charles P. McCormick of the Maryland spice business – and author of a book with the powerful title, *The Power of People*.

JURY METHOD – A way of forecasting sales, and a fairly primitive one at that. A group of executives produces estimates (or, more probably guesstimates) of what demand is likely to be, and somebody (usually the boss) decides what figures to run with. Alternatives with more basis in fact-finding as opposed to opinion include the "sales force composite method" (not much better), in which the sales people are asked for their estimates; in the "users' expectation method", you ask customers for their forecasts (much better, if there are only a few of the latter); and there is also (the best method) forecasting based on statistical information, and statistical method – such as "correlation analysis".

For instance, if the company knows the past relationship between world trade growth and air travel on international routes, an airline market forecaster can make a pretty good judgment from a global economic forecast. The more such correlations he has (with exchange rates, with fare levels, etc.), the better his forecast will be – though the risks of being wrong are still great. For that reason, sophisticated companies tend to use several methods – maybe all of them – in combination, in the hope of getting a better result. The forecasts may still come out wrong, but at least they've tried properly.

K

KANBAN – A Japanese word (which actually means "reminder") for a production and stock control system widely known as "just in time". The idea is that parts and materials arrive at the work station just in time for their use – instead of being called forth from a central depot where the components, etc. are held "just in case" they are needed.

The efficiency of the system is judged by its success in bringing down the number and size of the pallets or other containers circulating in the plant. Firms using *kanban* order only enough to replace the amounts being consumed – with no buffer stock on the line, and no warehouse worth speaking of. The conveyors are the only form of storage.

At pioneering Toyota, for instance, the computers give suppliers two to three weeks' notice of a production plan, specifying the component, the amount, the delivery time, and the order in which components are to be delivered. The reminder (the *kanban*) triggers the suppliers' response – but they don't actually let the deliveries go until they are actually required for the assembly line. Obviously, the suppliers can gear themselves to the same beautifully economical system.

You can't operate in this way, though, unless production throughout can be guaranteed to run smoothly. It isn't *kanban* that produces the uninterrupted and surprise-free operation of Japanese plants; it's the operation that produces the possibility of *kanban*. That doesn't make the Japanese less clever, though – it makes them look even more intelligent than Western managers whose sloppy production forces them to hold costly stock.

KEPNER-TREGOE – An approach to taking decisions and solving problems, and to training managers in how to do both. Devised by Charles H. Kepner and Benjamin B. Tregoe, the method is based on finding facts as the essential material for reaching decisions and solutions, but doing so in a disciplined, organised manner in successive stages.

KEY RESOURCES – Similar in concept to the critical or key success factor, the key resource is the one which gives a company the competitive advantage. Its corporate strategy thus plays to this resource – for instance, one common factor for an electrical goods firm might be its ability to manufacture motors at very low cost. It will seek to exploit this key resource by launching new products and product extensions that use the electric motors, while at the same time rationalising the design and manufacture of those power units to achieve the maximum economies of scale. The strategy is one of the most unsung aspects of Japanese business success. (*See also*: Critical Success Factor.)

KEY RESULTS ANALYSIS – The key result area is the part of some manager's job that is crucial to success (for the company as well as the manager). This is the core of an assessment and control method identifying all such areas in the job and laying down in hard terms what results are expected for the manager in each of the key areas (their number is seldom less than five or more than eight).

Everything, of course, must be set down on paper. The same phrase is used for the process of analysing the areas where success is essential for the corporation. The areas thrown up by key results analysis are the "key success factors" or "KSF". (*See also*: Critical Success Factor.)

KICKBACK – When jobs were scarce in the past, "kickback" most commonly meant the payment of part of your wages to the unprincipled operator who got you a job. Now, it's generally the payment, usually to a retail buyer, but also to industrial customers, of a sum of money in return for orders received. Strictly illegal, strictly against the interests of the buying firm (since it could have got an extra discount, and might have found a better, less corrupt source of supply). But it's probably the most prevalent form of business corruption in the Western world.

KISS – Stands for "Keep It Simple, Stupid" or, in the computer game, "Keep It Simple, Sir," when diplomacy is in order. In both cases, it refers to the principle that simplest is best, or, to put it another way, that if the solution you're adopting or the procedure you're following is complicated, it's probably wrong. Most management practices tend to get more complicated over time, partly because new forms, requirements, and checks and balances are loaded on top of those already in place. The only antidote is to keep on returning to scratch mentally, asking the question, "How would I set this up if I were starting with a clean slate?"

The KISS principle doesn't only apply to management procedures. It's also highly relevant to business planning and to organisation structures. The intellectual discipline is akin to that now demanded when value analysis is applied to product design. You reduce the business/organisation to the fewest, most integrated elements possible, and assemble them by the most direct means you can find. Thus, you don't muddle up a retailing operation with a manufacturing unit, or have one sales force selling two products with nothing in common, or insist on one unit reporting to two separate headquarters.

That's the KIS part of the acronym. But the S for Stupid in the rude version is important, too. It conveys the true and unforgettable lesson that, no matter how clever you are, or think you are, you will perform better in a simple situation than in a complex one. The over-elaboration which KISS is intended to kill often springs from managerial conceit, even from the desire to protect oneself by building an elaborate defensive mechanism around one's role. It's a policy that seldom succeeds in the end.

Look at most successful business strategies and tactics today (divestment, variety reduction, materials requirement planning, etc., etc.) and you'll find that, no matter how much complex technical jargon is used, it all comes down to one basic principle in the end: Keep It Simpler, Stupid. (*See also*: VA.)

KITING – Dishonest operators who are trying to keep together two ends that won't meet sometimes "kite" – they draw cheques on accounts they know to be empty in the hope that, by the time the cheque is presented, they can by hook or by (probably) crook get some money transferred into the account. They then draw another cheque on the account just emptied.

KONDRATIEFF CYCLE – The Russian economist Vassily Kondratieff constructed the furthest-ranging and most apocalyptic theory of trade cycles. Kondratieff cycles run for twenty-five to fifty years, a theory that fits quite well with the pattern of history. After being neglected as the long postwar boom seemed to prove him wrong, the dead Kondratieff came back into fashion after the 1973 oil price shocks. In Kondratieff theory the world won't emerge from a current down-phase in the cycle until 1995 – if not later. Judged by the frenetic business activity of the early eighties, you can tell that to the Marines, or, better still, to civilian participants in the early eighties boom. (*See also*: Trade Cycle.)

L

LABOUR-ONLY – A growing trend, especially in industries where the employment load is cyclical, is to subcontract the provision of labour to an outside contractor. While it's more expensive in one sense (since the contractor's profit has to be added to the cost of the labour), it's cheaper in another – the employer doesn't have to carry the cost of people he doesn't need, or the cost of firing the unneeded. In some trades (notably building) the contractor is the worker himself – who thus poses as a self-employed businessman.

LABOUR STABILITY INDEX – Divide the total of employees who have been on your payroll for a year or more by the total of all employees a year ago. If the ratio (the labour stability index) is 1, you've had total stability: if it's 50%, you've had terrible turnover, and there's something wrong with either you or the business. (*See also*: Turnover.)

LAME DUCK – Somebody or some corporation that doesn't or can't pay its debts. In Britain, commonly used for large companies that have been bailed out by the government and seldom succeed thereafter. The similar case of Chrysler in the United States proves that lame ducks can fly – sometimes.

LATERAL THINKING – Logical organisation isn't the only way of thinking, and may not be the best way – if the object of the thinker is to arrive at a brilliant, innovative, creative idea. The thinker and writer Edward de Bono has put forward the alternative approach of "lateral" thinking: the thinker ignores the straight-line reasoning of logical thought and looks instead for a literally far-out idea. In fact, from making the connection between two apparently unconnected thoughts, genuinely creative concepts may well arise. The name Apple is said to have been adopted for the computer only because the boss, Steven Jobs, was eating a piece of the fruit when nobody could think of anything else.

Lateral thinking is a training method as well as a tool for solving problems. You can make up your own mind on whether the lateral concept is any advance on the simple injunction to look for new solutions and new ideas, rather than stick with the old and stale. But certainly de Bono's notion has been a brilliant money-making lateral thought in its own right.

LAW OF DIMINISHING RETURNS – At first sight, this well-known and well-proven law of economics stands in grave contradiction to learning-curve theory. Where the latter holds that the more you produce, the more your real labour costs will fall, the law of diminishing returns lays down that after a certain point, more means less – i.e., the more you spend on trying to cut labour costs, the less the results will eventually be.

In fact, the results do diminish even under learning-curve theory – because the constant percentage fall in real labour costs which the theory predicts becomes a lesser and lesser absolute figure. But the law of diminishing returns applies more strongly and obviously where there's no gain from repetition. For example, in a programme to cut administrative costs, Pareto's Law will operate. Some 80% of the benefits will arise from 20% of the planned changes. It will therefore take 80% of the effort to get the last 20% of the savings – a truly diminished return.

The last 5% will be the most expensive and difficult saving of all. (Exactly the same phenomenon, incidentally, occurs in the training of athletes.) Knowing this law, an intelligent management has to decide when to sub-optimise, i.e., to seek the highest returns it can easily get, from a sales drive, say – or whether to go the whole hog: maximising the sales, but also maximising the cost. (*See also*: Learning Curve; Pareto's Law.)

LAW OF THE SITUATION – More often than not, people in business obey, not the law as laid down by some superior, but the requirements of what's going on – the "law of the situation", in the phrase produced by Mary Parker Follett (1868–1933). An extreme example is when a machine catches fire. The worker turns the fire extinguisher on the blaze because of the circumstances, not because the boss gives him an order.

Follett, one of the true and rare philosophers of American business, hoped to defuse the potential for conflict between subordinate and superior by common acceptance of the rational, justifiable grounds for a given course of action. Her human relations approach to management influenced the development of Douglas McGregor's Theory Y approach. It has only one obvious weakness. What if superior and subordinate disagree on the law of a given situation? There are no prizes for the answer. (*See also*: Human Relations School; Theory X & Theory Y.)

LDC – Less-developed country: a much politer sounding phrase than the older "backward economy" and an easier one to mouth than "industrialising country", another previous usage. The LDCs have lately figured mostly in agonised discussions about their huge debts to the West's banks, mostly those in the United States – or rather, about the LDCs' inability to finance these debts. But today's LDC can become tomorrow's prosperous challenger in world and domestic markets – witness countries in the Pacific Basin like South Korea.

LEADERSHIP – Once thought to be synonymous with managing, leadership has lost some of its lustre as the technical requirements of the management job have increased, and as the advise-and-consent aspects of man management have become more obvious and important. All the same, the leadership element in successful management can't be denied – what's more difficult is to define it.

The educationalist John Adair, though, has developed a training technique called "action centred leadership" which, building on ideas used in officer training in the military world, seeks to demonstrate that leadership can be learned, and isn't just a matter of inborn qualities. Adair's system adheres to his definition of leadership: carrying out the actions that are expected of a leader – a tautology if ever there was one.

LEAD TIME – How long it takes between placing an order and getting what you've ordered. From the viewpoint of the firm placing the orders, the lead time will determine its own timings – marking, for example, the critical stages in a network analysis. From the angle of the firm receiving the orders the lead time (unless it's maintaining a large stock of finished items, which is rarely a good idea) measures the time it takes to activate and complete the production cycle. Generally speaking, the shorter the lead time the more efficient the manufacture; but the longer the lead time . . .

LEARNING CURVE – The learning curve represents graphically what everybody knows from simple observation: that people get better at a task the more often they repeat it. The curve is of great importance in manufacturing, because if other things (like the cost of materials and energy) are equal (i.e., unchanged), the greater efficiency of labour will reduce overall costs over time.

Measurements of B-29 bomber production in World War II showed that with every cumulative doubling of output, the percentage fall in direct man-hours required was the same every time. The theory holds that the process never ends: that the line of labour performance holds to a steady improvement (although, of course, as the number of man-hours falls, the absolute saving becomes progressively smaller).

Manufacturing management and cost accountants must take this factor into account when making estimates of future costs. Otherwise, they could end up by overpricing, or (if wages are linked to output) overpaying. But the learning curve theory has acquired an importance even greater than that: the theory of the experience curve.

This holds that, like the individual operation, the whole corporation becomes more efficient at making any given product as its cumulative experience increases – and that its costs will go on decreasing as long as the object is in production. So far, so good. But one school goes on to conclude that the largest producer (cumulatively, remember) will therefore always have the lowest costs and thus the highest profits.

This theory, however, conspicuously fails to explain some of the major failures and successes of recent years; so the suggested strategy, of pursuing volume dominance of markets, to get price and profit dominance, while dropping all activities where cumulative experience is low, may simply be misguided. Anyway, technological change, with the accompanying sharp reduction in labour input, is making the argument increasingly academic.

LETTERBOX COMPANY – Usually in some place like Liechtenstein, the Cayman Islands, Jersey, or Bermuda – anywhere that charges little or no tax and has easy corporation laws. The genuine company that owns this unreal offshore convenience uses it mostly to reduce tax liability. All it requires in the locality is a letterbox and a reasonably honest lawyer to open the mail.

LICENSING – If you can't beat 'em, you have other options than joining 'em – you can buy from 'em, if their advantage happens to be a piece of technology or product that you need. The deluge of new high technology and the mounting cost of R&D have seen a big increase in the use of licensing, even by companies you might have supposed too powerful to have the need. Getting the right licences on the right terms (and granting them, for that matter) is a specialised business – one at which the Japanese proved adept at using in getting the industrial secrets they required by fair means as opposed to foul. (*See also*: R&D.)

LIMITED-LINE STRATEGY – What VW and Henry Ford got away with for as long as they could: keeping the variants to the product line to the minimum. Next to impossible in most modern markets – especially in cars, where today's trick is to generate the most apparent variants at the least added cost to the maker – and the highest added cost to the customer.

LINE – Several different meanings for a word that's vital in all of them. At its most basic, the line is the place where production takes place, possibly an assembly line, possibly not. Hence, line balancing (used to ensure that the workload on each station is equal), or line of balance (or LOB), which is the technique used to achieve line balancing by LOB diagrams and LOB networks.

In its second meaning, line is the antithesis of staff – terminology borrowed from the army. The people at head office are staff, for example, with no direct (or line) responsibility for production or marketing operations. These come under the command of line managers, the equivalent of field officers in the Army. In recent years, the balance of numbers and, in some aspects, of prestige, has swung from staff to line – partly because the work of line management (including running lines in the first sense of the word) has become more obviously the key to the success and survival of the corporation.

The third meaning of line is as in "line of command" – the route down which orders pass from the top to the bottom of an organisation. The currently fashionable approach seeks to make this line as short as possible. One way of doing this (and a good thing, too) is to reduce the number of staff managers between the chief executive and the line management.

That raises difficulties for the scalar principle, said to have been enunciated by Henri Fayol, the French pioneer of administrative management theory (*see* Control). This aspect of the organisation structure on which Fayol set such great store holds that the line of command must be a clear top-to-bottom chain of formal authority, with each link on a one-to-one basis: that is, each subordinate has only one superior – which must tend to lengthen the line.

Fayol's principle of "unity of command" is impossible to maintain in the complexity of modern businesses, with their matrix managements and rapidity of change. But a confused, unclear line of command is as dangerous today as in Fayol's time –

and always will be. (*See also*: Corporate; Chief Executive; Control; Matrix Organisation.)

LINEAR PROGRAMMING – In the days when computerised management science was a brave new thing, linear programming was one of the brightest new offerings – a method of optimising the allocation of resources when tackling a linear problem – such as how to transport goods around a distribution network in the most cost-effective manner, using the fewest vehicles and travelling least distance.

Problems of this nature are routine occurrences in business management, and their solution has become the same: routine, thanks to the development of linear programming techniques and their incorporation into the standard armoury of standard operational procedures – and thanks to the ubiquity of the computer.

LIQUIDATION – Literally, the conversion of assets that aren't liquid into those that are – cash or near-cash. The word is rarely used, though, for partial disposals, being reserved for wholesale jobs, voluntary or involuntary. Mostly, it's the latter variety, when a business can't pay its debts, and the creditors sell off the assets (or rather, a receiver does) to salvage what they can from the wreck (which usually isn't nearly enough).

The voluntary liquidation is theoretically a valuable element in capitalism: a company full of wealth decides to liquidate itself, and returns the proceeds to the shareholders, who are then free to invest in something new. In practice, managements will go to almost any lengths to keep their corporations intact, thereby (which is no coincidence) keeping their jobs intact as well. (*See also*: Credit.)

LIQUIDITY – As a wise man once remarked, liquidity is freedom, illiquidity slavery. A liquid investment is one (like a Treasury bill) that can readily be turned into cash. A liquid firm is one that can lay its hands on enough cash, at all times, to pay its bills. An illiquid company can't, and is thus at the mercy of bankers, creditors, and predators (who may be one and the same person).

LOGISTICS – While any commercial enterprise uses logistics, meaning the coordination of movement of manpower, materials, and goods so that all are available when and where needed, the science is especially demanding in overseas or remote projects. The logistics planner has to use networks and backup provision in a highly organised fashion if he doesn't want to end up with expensive drilling equipment and angry men stuck in the middle of the Sahara and unable to get out.

LRP – Long-range planning. Bears the same relationship to other planning (at least in the minds of its practitioners) as the College of Cardinals does to the bishops in the Catholic Church. Because the time horizon of the long-range planners is usually five years or more, it's somewhat difficult for them to be right. Also, it's rather difficult to prove them wrong, because, by the time the truth is out, they may be, too. In companies which, because of the long lead times in projects like building chemical plants, power stations, and oil refineries, are forced to look far ahead, the game of fitting precise numbers to far-off events has in many cases been superseded by scenario planning. In any event, the essential discipline of LRP isn't foretelling the future, which isn't given to man; the true discipline is thinking about the future in a concentrated, organised manner – which too many men don't do. (*See also*: Scenario Planning.)

M

MANAGEMENT – The definition that includes all the other definitions in this book and which, because of that, is the most general and least precise. Its concrete, personal meaning – the board of directors and all executives with the power to make decisions – is no problem, except for the not-so-little matter of where to draw the line between managers who are part of "the management" and managers who are not.

What managers of both groups, the ins and the outs, actually do is obviously management, but it covers so great a range of distinct activities that any broad, coverall definition is probably too broad. It's really three different overlapping sets of activities, which you might as well call short-term, medium-term, and long-term.

Short-term management is day-to-day, hour-to-hour, minute-to-minute: making things happen as they are supposed to happen and people behave as they are supposed to behave, or better still, exceeding the norms – getting higher output per man-hour, larger sales per call, faster processing of customers, and so forth. This is the bedrock of management, often entrusted to people far down the line but vital to success.

Long-term management, in contrast, is usually the prerogative of people right at the top of the line, the executive members of the board and anyone else they care to involve. It encompasses all the decisions about the corporation that will affect its future: the acquisitions and divestments, the top appointments and dismissals, the investment gos and no-gos, the plans and the planning structure, the organisation and reorganisation of the company, the development and deployment of personnel, the formation of objectives, etc.

Medium-term management is the bridge between short and long. It converts the plans and the objectives into the operational forms that short-term management then makes effective. This is the realm of budgets and projects, campaigns and programmes, financing and auditing, feedback and appraisal, etc.

Management thus adds up to the combination and coordination of short-, medium-, and long-term decision and execution in order to maximise the return on all the resources of the corporation over a sustained period of years. Neither science nor art, management draws heavily on both. Both inhuman (because it deals with the physical world) and human (because it uses people to satisfy the demands of people), management is a constantly shifting scenario – and good management, like the good corporation, is therefore a moving target, and a very difficult one to hit.

MANAGEMENT ACCOUNTING – Companies run on management accounts; they report in financial accounts. The difference is that management accounting is monthly, purely operational, and entirely internal: the financial presentation takes into account the financing of the business and all the indirect costs that cannot be charged direct to operations – and it doesn't need to be more than quarterly, if that. But if you want to know how the operations are really doing, it's the management accounts that tell the true story.

A typical set will show sales, itemised direct costs, and contribution. The accounts are also typically accompanied by supporting information (on, say, market share), which enables top managements to spot quickly what's going right – and wrong. The first figure they look for in main management accounts is the column called "variances". It's the large adverse gap between budget plan and actual outcome that sets alarm bells ringing – or should.

They should ring, though, well before the full set of management accounts is ready (no later than a month after the period being reported ends). Flash reports should go to higher management within a week of the month-end, to be followed by fairly accurate estimates a week or so after that. Nor is the object solely to alert, advise, and (maybe) alarm top management so that it can exert control. It's the manager of the unit concerned who most needs the figures, without which he can't know how he's doing – or perhaps what he's doing. (*See also*: Direct Costs; Contribution; Market Share; Variance.)

MANAGEMENT BY EXCEPTION – A born-again technique, first named by the great F. W. Taylor, who died in 1915. The idea is that managers should free themselves for the really important strategic and tactical tasks, the ones on which they should concentrate, by looking at day-to-day operations only when they show deviation from the norm – as in closed-loop systems.

The idea carries far more weight in the plant context in which Taylor worked than in wider areas of management. A machine can be assumed to be innocent of malfunction until proved guilty by variance from planned performance. An assembly operation, likewise, doesn't need intervention if the products are leaving assembly within standard costs, tolerances, and output rates.

But the division whose figures are right on target, or the salesman who regularly makes his quota, can't be taken for granted. Behind the perfect regularity may lie all manner of deadly deviations that will one day come tumbling out of the cupboard. Management by exception is thus an essential part of regular control systems. It's also something that all managers do automatically – select those areas where they'll spend their time and those they'll leave alone. But really effective management demands a different kind of management by exception: looking for trouble where all seems sweetness and light. (*See also*: Closed Loop; Standard.)

MANAGEMENT DEVELOPMENT – An organised activity within the corporation, aimed at bringing forward individual managers by providing them with new skills, a planned training programme, attitude and sensitivity training, etc. One step down in the hierarchy of personnel management institutions from organisational development. (*See also*: OD.)

MANAGEMENT GAME – A step or two beyond the case study method as practised at Harvard. The students are required to simulate the management of a real-life business situation, usually working as a team, with the score reckoned in pounds, often by the computer and with a time limit. A sometimes painful way of learning how to apply classroom lore under pressure – but also a painless way of learning that bad decisions lead to bankruptcy. (*See also*: Case Study.)

MANAGEMENT SCIENCE – Management isn't a science, but it can make highly intelligent and profitable use of science – and not in R&D alone. The possibilities of applying scientific disciplines to the business of management first became clear in World War II, when a British physicist, P. M. S. Blackett, demonstrated that the tools of his trade could be applied to the bombardment of Germany. That was the start of operational research – which is still an important management tool today, though not as important as its practitioners once thought it would become.

In fact, while the number of scientific techniques available to management has continued to expand, they are applicable to the narrow range of management problems – the ones you need to solve once the major decisions have been taken – or the ones you have to solve before you can take those big decisions. The computer has made it vastly easier to employ methods like simulation – but the management scientist remains a handmaiden to management, not the Philosopher King. (*See also*: OR; Simulation.)

MANAGERIAL GRID – One of the most popular management development systems, though looking a trifle old-fashioned these days. Devised by the team of Robert Rogers Blake and Jane Srygley Mouton in the sixties, the grid measures management behaviour on two axes – concern for people and concern for production. High concern in either department gets a score of 9;

low concern rates 1. You plot a manager's attitudes on the two separate 1-to-9 scales.

The hero of the grid is, of course, the executive with a "9, 9 managerial style" – the manager who strives his utmost to get the most, the best, and the richest output, but who also exhibits the greatest concern for the well-being and welfare of people who contribute to that production. In contrast, a "9, 1" style, concentrating on output and disregarding people, equates with Theory X: the authoritarian style.

As a training method, the grid is designed to make managers think about their styles, maybe to realise that their existing unsatisfactory combination is ineffective, and to lead them towards the goal of "9, 9". Whether the Grid itself is much use is a moot point. But there's no doubt of the value of being forced to examine how you set about the manager's ceaseless task of getting performance through people. (*See also*: Theory X & Theory Y.)

MANAGERIAL STYLE – It's a fairly recent notion, or bundle of notions, that (a) managers adopt patterns of behaviour towards each other – and, even more, their subordinates – which can be characterised; (b) that some of these styles are better – that is, produce better corporate results – than others; and (c) the style of a manager can be changed by training from a less effective to a far more successful variety.

The clearest definitions of management style are those used in the Blake–Mouton managerial grid, which is both a description and a training method – aimed at moving the trainee from a poor style (the worst being low concern for people combined with low concern for production) towards the best style (high concern for both people and production). But most other management training techniques do contain a large element of style-changing work.

That's obviously fundamental to sensitivity training, where the trainer seeks to develop the skills of people management. Style specifically concerns the relationship of the boss to his subordinates: and here the drift and drive of the times have been away from the autocratic style towards the more permissive, democratic, consultative variety. It's a movement that nobody can hope to stop – and nobody sensible would try to. (*See also*: Managerial Grid; T-Group.)

MAN-YEAR – The employment of one person for one year (just as man-hour is his or her employment for sixty minutes). While man-hours are useful only in calculating direct labour costs, man-years are the basis for planning total employment. Economy-minded companies are as miserly in allocating man-years as any Scrooge in shelling out his pennies. But it's a false economy to scrimp on man-years when the only result is to rob the company of the men and women it needs when they are needed.

MAPI – The Machinery and Allied Products Institute (MAPI) devised a formula to help companies decide whether it was worth buying new plant and equipment to replace what they already had. Given the origins of the formula, it wouldn't be surprising to find that the calculations generally come down in favour of buying replacements. Given the competitive conditions of today, it wouldn't be surprising to find that the formula was right, either.

MARGINAL – If you raise production or sales by one unit more, the costs associated with that increase are your marginal costs. If you use that figure in fixing the prices you charge for the extra amounts obtained, that's marginal costing, leading to marginal (or variable, or incremental) pricing.

Whether this is worth doing – i.e., selling the extra for less than you sold the bulk of production or sales – will be shown by the marginal income ratio. To find that, you divide the marginal revenue (what you get from the sale of that extra unit) by the net profit on the unit. The whole business can be a snare and a delusion, though. The marginal profit must bring down the overall profit ratio on the entire volume. That may not be so serious – unless the effect of the lower marginal pricing is to weaken the price structure for the whole product line.

The classic examples for marginal costing and pricing are airlines. Because there is no significant cost in carrying one more passenger, any fare, no matter how low, yields extra profit. Take it to its logical conclusion, though, and you get an airliner carrying only people from whom the company is earning a marginal profit, which may mean that the whole flight, perhaps the whole airline, is losing money, marginal hand over marginal fist.

MARKETING – This busiest of buzzwords in management is used, misused, and abused by managers all over the globe. Its proper understanding is essential to modern management – and that understanding is greatly helped by knowing how the "marketing concept" emerged. It came as a reaction to the long seller's market, during which producers simply manufactured what they wanted to make – not what the market wanted. Marketing turns that obsolete concept on its head, and the modern marketing tasks, to quote an expert on the subject, include:

"(a) Determining what the business shall make and sell, how many different lines and how many different sizes or patterns.

"(b) Determining the price at which the business shall sell them. Is it more profitable to sell x units at £10 each, or x plus fifty units at £8 each? This, of course, includes countless detailed decisions as to price policy.

"(c) Determining to whom the business can and should sell them. This, of course, involves market research and the development of new avenues and methods of distribution.

"(d) Determining when lines should be added or withdrawn. This includes the study of the demand so as to suggest directions in which the range may be improved, or to give an informed judgment on suggestions from other quarters. It also includes direct responsibility for seeing that the supply of new products is adequate both as regards frequency and design to secure the established market and the winning of new markets. It also includes all the detailed arrangements necessary to ensure that when a new line is launched the efforts of all departments of the business (design, production, advertising and selling) are united behind the new venture, focussed as to time, quantity, and range of effort.

"(e) If this duty is to be fulfilled satisfactorily, it involves a constant and systematic study of the products and methods of competitors.

"(f) Determining the quantities at which the business should aim in the sale of each of its lines. This involves economic study of general business trends, of the specific conditions and trends in given industry and enterprise, of local variations in general trends, and so on. From such studies should issue the general budget on which sales and production plans are based.

"(g) Determination of the standard of quality which the business should seek to maintain."

The only amazing thing about that indispensable short guide to what modern marketing means is that it was written by Britain's Lyndall F. Urwick in 1933. Do what he says fifty years on, and you should win.

MARKETING MYOPIA – The title of perhaps the most famous article ever published in the *Harvard Business Review*, by Professor Theodore C. Levitt. The shortsightedness referred to in the title was failure to perceive technological changes that would alter the basis of an industry and thus the fortunes of a company – with the most famous Levitt example being the buggy-whip manufacturers who failed to see the consequences of the horseless carriage. But Levitt also made the point that these companies (or US railways – also impoverished by the rise of the car) had failed to ask a vital question: What business are we in?

By one of those accidents of literature and life, marketing myopia has come to mean failure to ask and answer that question. The injunction to do so became one of the most persuasive and pervasive management precepts of modern times, leading many companies to enter into what proved to be strange and unsuitable diversifications as they sought to exploit their position in the wider businesses that they had now identified as their true occupation. The real, original meaning of marketing myopia is also likely to mislead, though, simply because technological forecasting (or TF) is so often wildly inaccurate – as Levitt has himself subsequently conceded. (*See also*: TF.)

MARKET LEADER – The time-honoured definition holds that the market leader is the firm with the largest sales. In general, this still holds true – but its corollary, that the largest sales are accompanied by the largest profits, has often ceased to apply, if the market is defined as the total sales in a given product or service area.

In these cases, profit leadership has passed to companies that lead, not in the overall market, but in a segment of that market. This isn't the case, however, where the overall market leader on volume takes care to remain the leader in quality, price, perceived value, cost – and all the other parameters that establish the boundaries of true leadership. (*See also*: Segmentation.)

MARKET RESEARCH – Organised, systematic investigation of markets and accumulation of relevant data. The most invaluable tool any manager can have in any market is one he can never possess – total knowledge of what's going on and why. What he can hope to obtain, though, is the answer to those questions that are truly vital. The art and craft of market research is to establish these questions and then, by a variety of methods, to obtain the answers.

Curiously, even those managers who use research (and many never do) are more apt to ignore the possibilities and prognoses of market research than to exploit them – the reason being that research findings often conflict with preconceptions, prejudices, and plans; since the prime purpose of research is to confirm or deny such propositions, the head-in-the-sand attitude makes no sense.

Another difficulty is that market research involves a plethora of techniques, much abstruse statistics, and several well-tried, trusty, and true principles that businessmen still find hard to accept: including the fundamental idea that a small sample can give an accurate picture of the buying habits of a large population. Polling, however, is only one of that multitude of techniques, and present purchasing habits are only one of the infinite number of subjects on which accurate or (equally important) stimulating information can be researched.

What price to charge; what kind of advertising to use; which medium to advertise in; which market to enter; with which product; how your company/products/service are perceived in relation to others . . . the list of possible questions is so long that a basic general management skill is to know what questions to ask the researchers to answer. An even more important ability, though, is that of making maximum use of their essential findings. (*See also*: Sample.)

MARKET SHARE – The vital indicator of a firm's penetration of a market – what proportion of total sales it accounts for. But beware: the statistic can be grossly misleading unless the market has been correctly defined. Anyone can limit a "market" so that his share of it looks good – and many do.

But even if the total market share does accurately reflect the company's position in its true market, that's not the end of the story. If the share is expressed in number of units, that may not correctly portray the share of total purchasing – a rival company may be getting higher prices. If the share is expressed in value, that may conceal the fact that the competitor is gaining unit volume by undercutting and is about to pounce on your previous share.

Then, how is your share holding up in relation to the largest competitors in the market? Or as a percentage of purchases by the largest outlets? In other words, market share is something you can't know too much about – and which you need to know a great deal about. (*See also*: Penetration Pricing.)

MATERIALS HANDLING – Has come more to the forefront of management concerns with the advent of automation. If you've got extremely expensive computer-controlled machines operating at great speed, you need extremely efficient, sophisticated handling systems to take materials into, through, and out of the plant. Highly automated equipment of this type is an essential ingredient of the factory of the future, or flexible manufacturing complex. In the most modern systems, the handling equipment can perform several functions other than transport: it can be the test bed on which essential testing procedures are carried out, and the only warehouse the factory really has – all the stock in an ultra-modern plant sits, not in some costly building, but on the conveyors. (*See also*: FMS/FMC.)

MATRIX ORGANISATION – A way of coping with the oldest problem in organisation – whether to have the company organised by function (such as manufacturing, marketing, personnel, R&D), or by product (for example, golf balls and meatballs), or by geography (the United States and Europe). Those who chose the functional route ran into the snag that the marketing director didn't actually sell either golf balls or meatballs, while the general managers for both kinds of balls (who did sell them) weren't responsible for the marketing decisions.

On the other hand, if all the functions were left to the golf-ball and meatball kings, poor coordination and duplication of effort tended to follow. Hence the matrix idea – first developed by NASA and its aerospace suppliers. The authority in the functional departments flows in the normal vertical manner, but the product or project is placed in the charge of a manager whose authority flows horizontally, cutting across the departmental frontiers.

The guiding principle is that responsibility for success is clearly located with the product manager, whose task includes drawing on the functional contributions without which he can't succeed. A famous example of matrix organisation is IBM, which organises its R&D globally, its manufacture by continent and its marketing nationally. Thus, a manager placed in charge of a research and development project in England is based in labs that are funded by corporate HQ in the United States; is employed by the national company in the UK; and is responsible for all aspects of the product (development, manufacture, marketing strategy, further evolution) as it gets introduced in the other national markets around the world.

The matrix system isn't simple to operate or establish – but, then, it's designed for complicated companies that would otherwise either be impossibly complex to manage, or which would fail in one way or other to realise their potential. Also, the matrix is a way of recognising that, in the modern business, clear distinctions can't easily be drawn, that boundaries exist to be crossed, and that you must find some way of combining the two highly effective but apparently opposed principles of maximising operational autonomy while also maximising the use of combined strengths. In its best applications, the matrix places every manager so that he has a single boss and a clear responsibility, but also a multiple role – all being necessary to make the most of today's challenges.

MBO – While the setting of objectives is essential for an effective company, management by objectives isn't. The MBO technique is only one way of seeking to control, coordinate, and motivate managers – and isn't necessarily the best. Starting from the top, the stages are (1) corporate objectives defined at board level; (2) management tasks analysed, with formal job specifications allocating responsibilities and decisions to individual managers; (3) performance standards set; (4) specific objectives agreed and set; (5) individual targets harnessed with corporate objectives; (6) management information system established to monitor achievement against objectives.

With all that put in hand, the MBO system is then supposed to get managers off and running, busily acting to implement and achieve their plans. The review mechanism enables the bosses to make sure that the above is happening – especially in the "key result areas" that are a strong feature of MBO.

Much else goes with it, such as management development, career progression, and salary review. Obviously, these activities take place in companies that have no MBO system or anything like it. Obviously, you can't run a proper budget system without setting objectives, and you can't run MBO without proper budgeting. But opinion has moved away from the idea of packing everybody into a formal system of objectives; today, when maximum flexibility is essential, achieving that rightly seems more important. (*See also*: Objectives; Key Results Analysis; Management Development; Budget.)

MDW – Measured day-work – a PBR (payments by results) scheme in which the bonus isn't paid by the piece, but by the amount by which the worker exceeds a standard level during the day. The idea is to combine the good features of piecework and the normal day wage – the first element providing the incentive aspect, and the second giving the stability of earnings that workers require for security of mind as well as pocket. (*See also*: PBR; Piecework.)

MERCHANDISING – You can take the retail horse to water, by getting him to buy your merchandise; but if you want him to drink, by actually shifting the goods, you have to merchandise: that is, you provide assistance that will encourage and enable the retailer to maximise the sales of your product.

The merchandiser's techniques run the gamut from point-of-sale advertising to in-store displays: tie-ins of retail promotions with ad campaigns in the media; part-financing of ad campaigns run by the retailer, but featuring the merchandiser's merchandise; and so on. It's an indispensable tool in hotly competitive consumer markets.

MIDDLE MANAGEMENT – If you're not in first-line supervision and you're not in top (or general) management, you must be in the middle – and a member of a threatened species. Each advance in the technology of management, especially in computerisation, has been hailed as the death-knell of middle management, but the genus has survived, even though, periodically, some overstuffed corporation sheds middle managers in droves.

This isn't because they are superfluous; it's only that they've chosen a sloppy employer. The increased complexity and scale of the corporation, together with the modern management mode of decentralising authority to discrete units, has greatly increased the necessity for and value of the middle manager. What's really called into question is the title – the status, in many companies, isn't any longer just a position in the organisation chart: it may be a crucial job like that of a product manager.

Anyway, in today's increasingly collegiate management, junior, middle, and top managers have been brought closer together in cooperative work aimed at optimising corporate results. The title "middle manager" still makes sense, though, if the middle is taken as meaning that the manager is at the heart of the corporation's affairs. He is. (*See also*: Product Manager; Collegiate Management.)

MIS – Advanced management information systems were the chimera of the seventies – computer-based marvels that would contain all the information any manager in the corporation wanted in order to make decisions, and that would feed it to him, in the form he wanted, over a terminal linked to a vast central computer. Whether this was a good idea or not, nobody will ever know. Nobody installed such a system (not even a computer manufacturer), and the idea was overtaken by new technology.

Now, the emphasis is on the "intelligent terminal" – another name for a personal computer, but one with access to the corporate database. This should give greatly improved information flows for decision purposes to levels far below the senior managements that were the intended beneficiaries of earlier systems. MIS can also be used for lower-level systems, providing real-time information for supervisors, say, to use in their work. But it's the higher-level meaning that carries the higher promise. (*See also*: DBMS.)

MISSION – The in-word in strategically driven companies for the tasks given to marketing units, plants, or R&D facilities. Typically, a company organised on the SBU principle (strategic business units) will give the unit managers missions. In multinational groups, internal competition to win missions is as powerful a driving force as competition with outside rivals – though winning the battle with the latter is, of course, the object of the mission, and of the whole exercise. (*See also*: SBU/SPU.)

MNC – Multinational company. Far back in the sixties, this was a badge of corporate honour, the mark of far-seeing managements whose ideas and organisations transcended national borders.

Some enthusiasts even saw the MNC as the key to a new world order of peace and prosperity. But in only a few years "multi-national" became a term of abuse and fear, especially for European socialists. The reason is probably that most MNCs weren't multinational at all – they were just very large American companies with sizeable overseas interests, dominated by American management.

Actually, in their subsequent years of unpopularity the MNCs have evolved, if slowly, in the very direction the optimists foresaw – with polyglot, interchangeable management from many countries and with some real increase in independence of the national companies. But there's still a long way to travel. (*See also*: TNC.)

MODELLING – The business model is becoming as ubiquitous as the economic one – the latter being the model that economic forecasters use in their prognostications. What's made modelling so common is obviously the spread of the computer, which makes it much easier to manipulate the equations that comprise all models.

These may not be very awesome pieces of mathematics: model $P = S - C$, for instance, indicates only that profit equals sales minus costs, and few thoughts are simpler than that. But building up all the relevant equations and establishing their interrelationships enables the complex modeller to simulate the operation of the entire company and to test for the effects of different decisions, competitive actions, changes in prices of materials, etc., etc.

While liable to be vastly less expensive than trial and error, simulation at the level of the company is subject to an immense range of possible errors – in the actual variables used and in the ways in which they relate. But at a lower level, modelling is now so routine that software packages for the simulation of the financial results of changes in the business can be bought off the shelf; many other routine aspects of the business (like stock or production control) can now (and should be) modelled to give the answer to the vital question, "What if?"

MONTE CARLO TECHNIQUE – As any business novice soon finds out, much that happens in real life, as opposed to the business-school environment, is strictly random. Pure or impure chance explains what occurs a great deal of the time – and you can no more predict those events than you can forecast which number is to come up when the dealer spins the wheel in a game of roulette.

Yet you still need to know what's *likely* to happen: for example, what the odds are on the same number coming up for a fourth time running. The answer has to be simulation. If you know what's happened in the past, you use the Monte Carlo technique to simulate the future – applying random numbers to the historical facts to get the future pattern of events into usable focus for decision purposes. If it matters, this only applies to a "probabilistic system" – which means a system where events are subject to outside and unpredictable influences. Since that definition includes every business that ever was or ever will be, you can see why Monte Carlo can help management. (*See also*: Simulation.)

MORPHOLOGICAL ANALYSIS – One of the more scientific (or pseudoscientific) methods of stimulating (or trying to stimulate) creative thinking. All solutions are a combination of alternatives – that is, to find the best route to a given destination, you need to know all the possibilities. The morphological analysis technique lists them in classes – that is, groups of mutually exclusive factors: if the first fork takes the road right or left, you can't choose both. Having classified the alternatives, you then try every combination of possibilities from each class to find the feasible and the best solutions.

MOTIVATION – The high priests of motivation theory (Maslow, Herzberg, McClelland, Vroom) all preach that humans can be led to perform more effectively if management presses the right buttons. The only trouble is that the priests disagree somewhat over what button to press. The general drift of the theories is the same, though: that you can't motivate so much by manipulating the basic requirements of the employee (for pay, job security, working conditions, etc.), as by activating the "higher" impulses.

These include things like seeking respect, obtaining promotion, making independent decisions, achieving desired outcomes. Probably the divisions between "motivators", like those between Theory-X and Theory-Y companies, aren't as rigid as the theorists make them seem. People get motivated by the whole employment package: but there's no doubt that such packages have been heavily influenced, and in the right humane direction, by the Mahomets of Motivation. (*See also*: Theory X and Theory Y.)

MRP/MRP2 – Material requirement planning means using information technology to keep stocks at the minimum efficient level – saving money and improving effectiveness in the process. It sounds complex and can demand computers – but the whole thing hinges round four simple questions, according to Oliver Wright.

1. What you gonna make?
2. What's it take to make it?
3. What you got?
4. What you gotta get?

Plainly you can't begin to answer the questions without an annual sales forecast. Plainly, the forecast is bound to be wrong – meaning that you have to alter the actual orders in line with changing demand as the reality unfolds. But because you've done the basic MRP work, the computer (or your hand, if the operation is small enough) can automatically do the adjustment to fit the circumstances, so you won't get stuck with too much stock – or too little.

Plenty of software packages now exist for MRP purposes. But in the way of the modern management world, MRP is outgrowing its own clothes. To the insiders, the initials now mean "manufacturing resources planning", or MRP2. The system does for the manager something akin to what the genie in the bottle did for Sindbad the Sailor – everything he wants. To quote two *Management Today* authors, that includes "maintaining physical stock records; accounting for inventory movements; planning the requirements for raw materials and intermediate components; also, planning and monitoring the use of productive facilities (both labour and machines) and available capacity; monitoring actual costs; drawing up schedules for the use of the purchasing department; controlling work in progress; and following manufacturing variances".

What MRP2 gives you is the equivalent of an airline's seat reservation network: an on-line, on-screen system that gives instant access to the condition of stocks, orders, and facilities, and lets you plan them as long in advance as you need – which is a lot longer than companies used to plan before the computer came along.

This isn't an overnight job, though. MRP2 takes time, and if it takes too much time, the whole thing can be blown. Hearken to four-question Oliver Wright: "Because MRP requires a concentrated effort to install, it's important to install it in a minimum amount of time ... It's important that a company try to take eighteen months or less, since it's difficult to keep management's attention for any longer period . . ." He can say that again.

MSA – Multiple scenario analysis. A close relative of the scenario approach to economic forecasting. The strategic planner using MSA lists all the possible scenarios, with all the possible combinations of variables. He then decides which of the combinations are plausible and which are not. The task is to devise the right strategy for each plausible scenario, leading up to the final choice of the single strategy which best covers all the possibilities: that is, gives the optimum response. Whether it is the optimum response, of course, no one will ever know. (*See also*: Scenario Planning.)

MULTIPLE BRANDING – When a company sells basically the same product under different brand names, all competing with each other. The classic example is General Motors, with much the same car masquerading under the Chevrolet, Pontiac, Buick, and Oldsmobile labels. The technique works well as long as you're not facing serious competition from outside, as GM did in compact cars from the Japanese – which was the reason for the giant's giant shakeup of 1984, reestablishing the brands as separate identities, competing not with each other but with the great world beyond.

MURPHY'S LAW – "If anything can go wrong, it will." This cynical view of human affairs is, unfortunately, absolutely right: if the possibility exists for an assembly, a fitting, a repair, to be done wrongly, the time will come (probably sooner rather than later) when that is exactly what will happen – witness the Three Mile Island nuclear disaster. The corollary of Murphy's Law is therefore that effort spent on anticipating what could go wrong is invaluable – since the expense of incurring and correcting the damage (as at Three Mile Island) will vastly exceed the cost of prevention. This is a basic discipline in risk management. (*See also*: Risk Management.)

N

NET – What's left of anything after deducting what must be deducted. Applied to assets, that means deducting from the total all current liabilities. Applied to current assets, it means deducting those same current liabilities to get a net sum that equals working capital – work in process or progress, stocks of materials and parts, consumable items, what customers owe the business, and any cash or near-cash you've got in the bank.

Applied to profit, net is what you get after deducting from the trading or operating profit all the financial charges – bank and other interest, etc. There's also net worth – which means the same as equity. It's all the ordinary shares plus all the reserves and retained profit. Since balance sheets must balance, that should equal the total of the net assets. If it doesn't, the accountants are terribly wrong – or something else is. (*See also*: Current; Working Capital.)

NET BENEFIT-COST RATIO – You can do this sum two different ways. Either way, you have to calculate the expected annual cash inflows and outflows from a project, including depreciation. You can express the resulting numbers as a ratio of each other, just like that – "undiscounted". Or you can discount the numbers by working out the PV (present value) of the inflows and outflows: that is, you devalue each set of figures by a chosen rate of interest – dividing them into each other then gives you another ratio by which to judge the attractions (if any) of the project. (*See also*: Depreciation.)

NETWORK – Any project or operation is composed of a number of events all taking place at various times. The relationships between times and events form a network that can be presented graphically; these drawings are the basic tools for planning and managing projects.

NET WORTH – Another phrase for shareholders' equity or invested capital – what belongs to the owners of the ordinary shares, as opposed to what belongs to the bankers and others who have lent money to the company. Hence the "net": the loans are deducted from capital employed to arrive at the worth (or supposed worth). (*See also*: Capital.)

NICHE – Not so long ago, a niche was something you put a treasured vase in. Now it's the treasured word of managements great and small. The niches at which the executives aim are areas of the market where (preferably) nobody else competes, but where, by offering a unique product or service and deploying unique skills, the niche exploiter can find rich pickings.

The classic niche was that found by BMW when nigh unto death. It sought to establish itself between the might of Mercedes and the massive size of VW. By concentrating on cars for the executive who wanted something sportier than a Merc and smarter than a VW or Audi, BMW became the most successful car firm of its era – if you judge success by profits and expansion.

The "niche" is obviously a variant of "segmentation". The difference is that the niche marketer concentrates on the segment he has identified and deliberately avoids moving into other segments where he'll find competition. The catch is that as marketing changes, so can the masonry around the niche – with serious impact on a firm like Digital Equipment. Its niche, minicomputers, lost its loveliness because of (1) more effective competition in minis from IBM, which once hardly figured in DEC's niche; and (2) the rise of the microcomputer, which could do much of the mini's work. DEC was forced to leave the former safety of its niche and compete in the much tougher conditions of the micro market.

Though such cautionary tales abound, so do niche opportunities. The segmented, specialised markets of today demand segmented, specialised suppliers – who may not stay small for long. The fact is that DEC became the world's second largest computer company, with sales of $4 billion. That's some niche. (*See also*: Segmentation.)

NIH – Not invented here – the standard (and stupid) response to any idea that hasn't originated in the company – or sometimes the department – concerned. The stupidity is gross because of the strong possibility that other people, approaching the problem from another angle, have come up with a better solution – or at least a solution that is worth investigating, both in its own right and as a stimulant to further and different development of the basic idea.

NIH used to be especially strong in departments involved in R&D. The proliferation of technological advance, plus the convergence of different technologies, has made this stance especially difficult to maintain. Hence the rise of licensing and other arrangements for sharing or exchanging technology. What's true in the labs, though, applies equally strongly in other departments of the company. NIH is a symptom of closed minds and resistance to change. These days, no company can afford either. (*See also*: R&D; Licensing.)

NPV – *See* IRR.

O

OBJECTIVES – As a management term, this word has become one of the most powerful and universal of them all – thanks in large part to the teaching of Peter Drucker. His insistence that both companies and individual managers must have targets at which to aim has animated innumerable businesses and influenced the development of many techniques – especially in the areas of motivation, remuneration, and planning.

Whether or not the company uses the most fully developed scenario, which came to be called management by objectives (or MBO), it's necessary for the board (or the chief executive on its behalf) to form corporate objectives, which may well not be expressed in figures. Example: to obtain the leading position in the South-East in the agricultural chemicals market. Another example: to improve the company's reputation for reliability and quality to the highest level in the industry.

But such objectives, to become meaningful, have to be rephrased into specific tasks, to which specific numbers can often be attached. The tasks (objectives) will then be broken down as they descend to divisional, subdivisional, and finally operating level. At all stages, meeting these divided and subdivided objectives for the corporation becomes the objective of the individual manager. If he's the unit boss, the unit's objectives and his own main targets will obviously be one and the same.

But the manager should have other targets all his own – like developing so many (a precise number) junior managers capable of promotion to other jobs, including his own. In all the above uses, objectives are planning tools for binding the whole organisation and its management together to achieve common purposes. In itself, that's highly motivational; at the personal level, meeting objectives or hitting targets is a well-known and strong motivator – and not in business alone.

Also, the agreement of objectives by manager and subordinate gives a reasonably solid basis on which the latter can receive appraisal. Better still (some think), you can tie remuneration to meeting the objectives. Make your numbers, and you make your bonus. Don't, and you don't. In fact, some such principles drive most companies, whether they know it or not and whether they formalise it or not.

Budgets enshrine objectives, after all, and you don't generally reward people for not doing what they're supposed to. But clarity about objectives is an enormous step forward for everybody, even if you prefer (like most companies) not to use the targets as the basis for a formal, maybe too formal system for managing your managers. (*See also*: MBO; Appraisal; Budget.)

OD – Organisation development is one of the most ambitious efforts of personnel managers to get a stranglehold on power. The OD activity seeks simultaneously to develop individual managers and to improve the organisation's ability to attain its goals. The methods employed include a great deal of coaching and objective-setting; but OD has generally been seen as too cumbersome to please anybody except the personnel people in charge, and it's not difficult to see why.

OD's proponents argue, however, that individual approaches like the managerial grid, sensitivity training, and management by objectives (MBO) constituted only a piecemeal approach to improving effectiveness. OD, in contrast, is a comprehensive process, starting with (1) establishing a company philosophy; (2) long-range planning (LRP); (3) establishing short- and long-term objectives for every division and unit in the company; (4) organisational planning and restructuring; (5) changing the organisational climate and management style – which is where the grid, sensitivity training, T-Groups and so on come in; (6) management systems – here MBO may come in; (7) work organisation, equipment, and methods – the nuts and bolts of the business. As you can see, that doesn't leave much of the company or its management untouched. Which makes the point that effective management of itself develops the organisation – continuously, not as an OD programme. (*See also*: Managerial Grid; T-Group; MBO; LRP; Objectives.)

OEM – Original Equipment Manufacture. When a tyre company supplies tyres to Ford to put on a new car, that's OEM business – manufacturing an item, maybe the whole thing, for another manufacturer who will actually market the goods. The business is getting wider and wider; even proud names like IBM are heavily involved in OEM, both ways. One reason is that no companies today can hope to make every high-tech assembly from their own resources. Another reason is that OEM (even for a rival company) is one way for a company to make the most money from its key resources. (*See also*: Key Resources.)

OFFICE OF THE FUTURE – The ultimate in information technology: the office stuffed with all the latest smart equipment, from PABXs (private branch telephone exchanges), through the whole range of electronically operated aids: electronic typewriters, photocopiers, telephones, switchboards, key systems, word processors, computers, viewdata, telex, teletex, printers, modems, digital storage, local area networks, dictating machines, paging, laser disks, microfilms, keyboards, fax systems ... and much, much more. It's not just that these gadgets cover every imaginable need in the office: by communicating with each other, and with their cousins in offices anywhere else in the world, the devices will provide managers with the dream, the ideal, the Holy Grail – instant communication, instant information and instant processing of data on a global network. That, at any rate, is the dream. Who knows? It might even become reality.

ON COST – Means the same thing as indirect costs: the expense that's on your back (or over your head) before you've made or sold a single unit.

OPERATING PROFIT – Similar in meaning to trading profit, and a number that should correspond fairly closely to added value. It's the surplus earned from normal operations – that is, the difference between revenue and operating expenses in the main commercial activities of the firm, before deducting financial charges, such as interest costs. Since the calculation excludes some central costs over which divisional and subdivisional managements have no control, operating profit is often used as the basis for financial targets and performance review. It's a number that can dwindle away with amazing speed once the accountants get their hands on it. (*See also*: Profit; Added Value.)

OPPORTUNITIES – The O in SWOT. Any good company with alert and aggressive management will have more opportunities than it can possibly handle with the available resources. This doesn't refer to opportunity in the familiar, common sense of "opportunity knocks", but rather to a quite technical definition of the profitable options available to a company, given its existing complement of financial, marketing, manufacturing, and manpower strengths, together with those strengths it can obtain, if the opportunity requires their possession.

Every business should regularly review its opportunities – and every businessman should remember that the ones that get away have included some of the biggest bonanzas of the twentieth century. Thus Eastman Kodak, though it was so gigantic in one kind of image making, didn't spot the opportunity presented by another form, xerography, when the inventor came calling. Thus Xerox in turn, when the Japanese began making smaller copiers, didn't spot that as an opportunity and was fatefully late in responding. A missed opportunity, as in that instance, can become a serious threat. (*See also*: SWOT.)

OPPORTUNITY COST – This doesn't mean how much money will be required to take an opportunity. It means how much money you've *lost* by taking one. The unavoidable fact is that, since resources are always finite, spending £X million on one course of action means that you're not able to take an alternative one.

If the alternative would have produced a higher return, then the "opportunity cost" is the difference between that figure and what (if anything) you actually earned in the chosen activity. At first glance, it might seem stupid to take the least remunerative option. But sometimes you really have no choice – when, for example, an old profitable product is replaced, for sound marketing reasons, by a new one on which initial losses will certainly be made.

As that example shows, the opportunity-cost calculation isn't of much practical use, except in one very important respect. If you calculate "opportunity cost" simply as the interest foregone by not investing the funds, or the earnings lost by not employing the capital in your business at its current yields, you rub in the point that money (even your own money) costs money.

That's a valuable way of reminding managers – especially, say, when contemplating some inadvisable merger – that they're paying even more for the fancied company than they believed. On the other hand, taken to absurd lengths, the "opportunity-cost" principle would stop managers from doing almost anything. In some cases, that might be a good idea, but not in all.

OPTIMISATION – You can't get the best of both worlds: but the best management tries. These days, it's greatly helped by the computer, which is brilliant at working out the sums that show, for example, which combination of output and stock levels will produce the optimum result for the company.

The point is that the optimum level for the product people (normally producing to near the limit of capacity) will be disastrous if the output merely goes into stock; whereas achieving the optimum level of stock (the lowest possible) might raise unacceptable consequences for manufacturing – and risk impossible sales losses for marketing.

Actually, all business activities are subject to the optimising principle, since the coordination of different activities and objectives always means some sacrifices. You can't generally go for the maximum volume at the maximum price, for instance. The secret is to find the price level which, when combined with the expected level of demand, will give the best result on the bottom line.

Such calculations are bread and butter to marketing planners. But the pressures of reality mean that events seldom work out perfectly – most businesses are subject to sub-optimisation most of the time. But the better businesses strive all the time to reduce that sub-optimised element: to optimise it, in fact.

OR – Operational research. This discipline, which came into its own in World War II, uses all available scientific and (above all) mathematical techniques to solve operations problems – in the wartime context, for example, how best to organise convoys or bombing raids. The operational researcher aims to break away from subjective answers and to produce only objective ones supported by verifiable data.

ORGANIC GROWTH – Expansion of the existing businesses of a company, or development of new business within the company, rather than expansion by takeover or merger. The latter can be used to accelerate and assist organic growth, but obviously the purchase of another company doesn't in itself constitute growth in a meaningful sense.

ORGANISATION AND METHODS – Organisation and methods, the equivalent of work study in the factory, is applied to the administrative functions of the corporation. The O&M specialist sets out to get higher efficiency from office staff and systems by analysing what's being done and comparing it to what could be done if methods and organisation were changed.

As the computer has spread its tentacles, so the O&M people have widened their sphere to cover EDP (electronic data processing), going deeper and deeper into the bowels of the business. They can be a nuisance, but their basic principle – that every clerical/administrative function can and must be improved – is clearly right. (*See also*: Work Study.)

OVERTRADING – It's as easy (if not easier) to go broke by selling too much as it is by selling too little. In the second instance, so long as the unlucky businessman doesn't buy or produce more than he's able to sell, he can keep going for a surprisingly long time. In the first instance, though, a business that greatly expands sales will also greatly expand the expense of sales – and that can be a fatal trap.

The trap opens if the gap between the two flows of cash (in and out) becomes too large. Normally, the expenses of sales (including wages and supplies) have to be met before the income from sales is received. If the business expands too rapidly, it simply runs out of ready cash, can't meet its bills, and collapses.

Some forms of business are (or should be) immune to the disease. Typically, in supermarkets and other non-account retailing a businessman gets credit from his suppliers but gets paid on the nail by his customers. If you're not that lucky, you can try to make your luck – Henry Ford, when the banks attempted to put the squeeze on him, broke free in a single bound by making Ford dealers deposit cash in advance if they wanted more cars. But never rely on suppliers' credit as a source of capital. Businesses sometimes do that when their own capitalisation is inadequate. The company that relies on suppliers' credit when undercapitalised skates on thin ice – and is in grave danger of falling through the ice if rapid expansion forces it into overtrading. (*See also*: Capitalisation.)

P

PARALLEL IMPORT – Whenever a firm tries to maintain higher prices in one export market than in another market (usually but not always the domestic one), it opens the door to possible parallel or "grey" imports brought in by somebody else. It's a form of industrial arbitrage. The parallel importer undercuts the main importer on price, and can be a terrible pain in the neck. (*See also*: Arbitrage.)

PARETO'S LAW – The famous 80–20 rule, set out by a 19th century Italian economist, is basic to better management. Pareto observed that in any series, a small proportion accounted for a large share of the outcome; hence the law's description: "the significant few and the insignificant many". Translating that into business terms, 80% of a firm's profits will come from 20% of its products; and 80% of its sales from 20% of its customers.

Analysing a business in this light shows the management where to concentrate its efforts – and, very possibly, which customers to drop and which product lines to cast into outer darkness. But the usefulness of Pareto's Law doesn't stop there. It also tells you that 80% of the value of your stock will be accounted for by 20% of the items held: that 80% of the costs of an assembly will be accounted for by 20% of the components – and, again, this analysis is an essential guide to action.

Concentrate on tight control of the significant 20% and you will achieve vastly greater savings than from effort wasted on the insignificant 80%. The principle is very important in operating schemes like quality circles: you don't want to waste people's time working on problems whose solutions won't make much contribution to the overall result. On the same argument, management ought to watch its own use of time carefully, to ensure that it is concentrating on the vital, not (as happens ridiculously often) on the trivial.

You'll *always* find, on checking, that a Pareto distribution applies – although managers often find it difficult to accept the truth that so much of their effort is relatively futile. Even pay structures tend to follow the law, with the top and bottom pay determined less by greed at the top than by a mathematical relationship. But there are a couple of warnings needed: first, 80–20 isn't a golden mean – the proportions will vary, though the principle won't; second, you can't go on indefinitely chopping out the insignificant many – otherwise, sooner or later, there won't be anything much left at all. Even in the most perfectly efficient company, with the ideally balanced product portfolio and customer profile, Pareto's Law will still apply. The only difference is that the perfection and the ideal will have come about in part by making use of its invaluable guidance.

PARKINSON'S LAW – Little did *The Economist* know, when it published an anonymous essay by a professor based in Hong Kong, that it was adding a potent new phrase to the worlds of business and politics. The theme of the piece was that "work expands so as to fill the time available for its completion"; and its title, "Parkinson's Law", slightly breached the paper's traditional anonymity – Cyril Northcote Parkinson being the author.

As a book, the thesis became a world best-seller – not so much, actually, for the law itself as for some of Parkinson's other insights into the ways of the bureaucratic world: notably, the tendency for office empires to proliferate unless or until somebody stops them. Parkinson had great fun demonstrating how the British Admiralty had swollen as the numbers of ships and sailors in its care had shrunk.

"Parkinson" has become the standard word for a phenomenon

that can be seen at its expensive work in every establishment created by corporate man. In another book, *The Law and the Profits*, Parkinson came up with another law: "Expenditure rises to meet income." This, too, rang an instant bell with perceptive managers, who spotted that what is certainly true of governments (and helps to explain the traumas of cutting government deficits) also applies to companies.

The observation encouraged the rise of disciplines like zero-based budgeting, which seeks to cut spending plans loose from available funds (i.e., what was spent before) and to relate them to actual need. Parkinson's insight was presumably influenced by his own aversion to high taxation. Practising what he preached, he took himself and his royalties off to the nearly tax-free isle of Jersey. (*See also*: ZBB.)

PARTICIPATION – "Participative management" came into vogue in the late sixties, as traditional top-down management appeared to be running afoul of the changed attitudes and reactions of a better educated, more demanding work force. The preferred remedy for the diseases of worker alienation and its symptoms of low productivity and high absenteeism was (to the joy of social scientists) worker participation.

It can take two forms, not mutually exclusive. Participation in ownership gives the workers shares in the corporation, and thus a shareholder's voice in the conduct of its affairs. Participation in decision making gives the workers a say in those affairs, usually only over matters that directly affect their interests – like working hours or plant closures. The most publicised experiments in participative management have taken place in Sweden. The Volvo factory at Kalmar, for instance, was planned with the active participation of the workers. Formed into small groups each responsible for a complete assembly, they fixed their own work schedules and other tasks. While more expensive than traditional car industry practice, the system was designed to recoup the cost through lower absenteeism and higher quality.

Under West German law, through a system of works councils, participative management has become obligatory for firms above a certain size; and the European Commission has been pushing for years to spread it through the Common Market countries. Interest in and enthusiasm for participation waned after the oil strike of 1973, though, as cost cutting, higher productivity and job preservation took over in the forefront of managerial minds.

In recent years, participation has been coming back in a revised form. Instead of decision making, the new participatory groups concentrate on working methods – on ways of improving general operating efficiency, under names like "quality circles" or QWL ("quality of working life"). The idea, stimulated by the Japanese example and still more by Japanese inroads into Western markets, is to increase pride in one's work as well as performance on the job. It does, too. (*See also*: QC; QWL.)

PAYBACK – Old-fashioned this method of investment appraisal may be, but it tells you one thing you positively must know – when you're going to get back the pounds spent on your investment project. It's very simple – just divide the capital cost of a machine, say, by what it will earn or save (before depreciation) in a year.

The answer, as for a £200,000 machine yielding £50,000, will be expressed in years – in this case, four (probably too long). The objection to payback is that it says nothing about the return on the investment over its entire life. So it's customary to use other, newer methods (such as investment appraisal) for this purpose. But when no less an expert than Peter Drucker recommends that you combine these later techniques with payback, it's very foolish not to accept the advice. (*See also*: Depreciation; Investment Appraisal.)

PBR – Payment by results. The controversy will never die over whether payment should be made for results or should be "a fair day's pay for a fair day's work", in the old phrase. The balance is tilting right away from straight PBR, simply because so many more workers are now in the knowledge or service industries where PBR is far more difficult to apply.

In addition, many schemes (such as the Scanlon Plan) seek to get the best of both worlds, guaranteeing the worker a secure and stable wage, but obtaining maximum output by bonus schemes tied to productivity targets – to be met not by the individual but the group.

PBR schemes can also be group based, with the team rather than the worker earning more in relation to the actual output achieved. The sheer number of different PBR programmes is evidence of their difficulty: they need constant revision to ensure that management is neither overpaying for the output it's getting nor getting less output than it requires.

The Barth system is one such scheme. Before even starting, you need to know the standard time for a unit of output (a), set a standard rate of hourly pay (b), then count the individual's output for a period (c), and the hours he actually worked (d). Then, so Carl George Lange Barth decreed, you multiply $a \times c \times d$; take the square root of that and multiply it by b, the hourly rate.

There has to be an easier way to earn somebody a living. If complex arrangements are necessary, so current opinion holds, it's better to use them for an overall scheme of incentives – one (such as the Bedaux system) involving everybody, and not just those whose work can be counted in units. (*See also*: Scanlon Plan; Standard.)

PDM – Physical distribution management is one of the Cinderellas of the business game: desperately important, a major item in everybody's costs, a high-potential route to both economies and more effective marketing; but unglamorous, and relegated far down most corporate pecking orders. So anybody who wants to and can achieve the most deliveries with the fewest vehicles and route miles has a great advantage in prospect.

The computer has made it far easier to work out and get close to the optimum system. But management can't achieve the optimum without rationalising the network of customers to whom deliveries are made and the network of places from which the deliveries start. This in turn demands a marketing strategy – concentrating on key accounts, say, and dropping customers who require uneconomic loads or excessive journey-time. Rethinking the marketing strategy with PDM in mind can lead not only to more effective marketing but also – as a sensational by-product – to substantially higher profits. (*See also*: Rationalisation.)

PE – Price-Earnings Ratio. Divide the profit (computed after all tax, interest, minority interests, etc. have been deducted) by the number of ordinary shares in issue and you get the earnings per share. Divide that number into the day's stock market price, and you get the PE. When the PE is astronomical (80, say), it's usually because the City expects a stratospheric rise in future earnings. When the PE is abysmally low – in single figures – the City is predicting slumps, losses or worse.

Note that in either case (unless bad or good news has actually been revealed, a quadrupling of sales or a plant closure involving a massive write-off), predictions, expectations or forecasts are involved. So there's an inevitable and high risk of error. The only PE which is certain is the historic one, based on the previous year's earnings. The prospective PE – that is, the figure actually being earned right now, or that might be earned next year – can only be estimated by outsiders with varying degrees of accuracy (or inaccuracy).

Also, because the share price is discounting this present and future growth when the PE is high, it doesn't follow that the achievement of the expected earnings will be followed by a further rise in the price of the shares – let alone in the PE. All shares with high PE's eventually suffer drastic re-rating – that is, their ratios retreat towards the norm, which can inflict terrible breakage on investors' nest-eggs. At the other end of the scale, chances are always better than the market thinks that a low PE will rise towards that same market norm; and the results of that up-grading, financially speaking, can be entirely delightful.

PENETRATION PRICING – One way of knocking out competition before it even starts is to set so low a price that nobody else can enter the market at a profit. The strategy won't work, obviously, unless the knock-out attempt is backed by large volume – needed both to achieve low costs and to preempt customer purchases.

Achieving penetration in this way was easier before development and launch costs became so steep. More typically today, the innovator relies on novel product attributes to get market penetration, only bringing the price down as volume rises and costs reduce. When Texas Instruments, having used the above strategy with enormous success in microcircuits, tried straight penetration pricing in microcomputers, the result was catastrophic: TI couldn't match the volume or the costs of Commodore, and the only thing penetrated by its low prices was TI's own profitability.

PERCEIVED VALUE – What purchasers believe they are obtaining for their money. The days when lowest price equalled highest value in the mind of the purchaser have long gone. On the contrary, low price is instinctively equated with lower quality, while a higher (premium) price is linked with higher quality. If the difference in quality perception is greater than the difference in price, then the product has a higher perceived value – which is all that matters.

To illustrate and emphasise the point, IBM's Personal Computer was more expensive on its arrival in the market than existing products that were technically either better or its equal. But the IBM branding gave the product a higher perceived value, which made it a smash hit. In contrast, the smaller PC Jr, lacking some features that purchasers expected, couldn't achieve the same perceived value and was a flop.

PERFORMANCE REVIEW – The form of appraisal used in MBO – management by objectives. It's the meeting where superior and subordinate get together to review the latter's performance and agree on a new JIP (job improvement plan) to achieve still greater wonders in the future. (*See also*: Appraisal; MBO.)

PERPETUAL INVENTORY – Doesn't mean that stock is kept in the warehouse for ever – though if you looked into some warehouses, you'd think it was. All that perpetual inventory means is that you update the stock records continuously, so that you always know what's gone out, what's come in, and what's held in the store.

Before the computer came into its full glory, maintaining a

perpetual inventory was impossible in an even reasonably complex company. Now, it's child's play. With the development of "just-in-time" – or *kanban* – methods, there's so little stock held at plant level that keeping a perpetual account of it is hardly worth the bother. The warehouse (or PDC: physical distribution centre) is less like a store, more like a pump: pumping in materials and components at one end and pumping them out at the other in a continuous or – if you will – perpetual cycle. (*See also*: Kanban.)

PERT – Programme evaluation and review technique (to give the whole mouthful) was the pride and joy of the US Navy's Special Projects Office. The purpose is the same as that of the critical path method (CPM): in planning projects, to analyse the network of activities to establish the critical path of events whose delay will delay everything. Booz, Allen & Hamilton Inc., the management consultants, were deeply involved in devising the technique, which rests on an intriguing approach to estimating.

The planner makes three estimates ("most optimistic", "most likely", and "most pessimistic") for how long each activity will take. He then divides the most optimistic time by six, adds to that the most likely time multiplied by four, and adds to that total the most pessimistic time (not multiplied or divided). The result is the "expected elapsed time", which is what the planner puts on the "*activity on arrow*" diagram of the network, and which is also what he uses to fix the critical path.

Although the use of PERT and its various variations is confined largely to the planning of complex projects, its principles are basic to all efforts to apply logical thought to physical activities. It was the first of the postwar innovations in management technology to capture attention, and although it rapidly lost its early glamour, the PERT approach is earning its keep – and improving corporate fortunes – somewhere every day of every year. (*See also*: CPM.)

PETER PRINCIPLE – Does every employee in a hierarchy tend "to rise to the level of his own incompetence"? The answer is none too clear, but people plainly want to believe the theory, which made the book *The Peter Principle*, named after Laurence J. Peter, and written by him with R. Hull, into a best-seller. The theory was believed most strongly of business organisations, although Peter himself is an educationalist, whose theory is said (understandably) to have been based on experience in the California school system.

What makes the Peter Principle so appealing to managers (and to management's critics) is that it provides a theoretical justification for the feeling that those in power or authority are no good – since the higher people rise, the nearer they come to the level at which they cease to be competent. It also fitted the well-known phenomenon of overpromotion – in which, for common example, a great salesman becomes a hopeless sales manager.

Apart from alerting management to such dangers, though, the Peter Principle is not of great practical use. But its debunking attitude has certainly helped to encourage an irreverent attitude towards hierarchies. Peter showed excellent timing – for his book appeared at just the time when hierarchy as an organising style was slipping off its pedestal. Peter gave it a valuable push. (*See also*: Hierarchy.)

PHANTOM STOCK – An incentive scheme that rewards employees with units, representing stock either in the company or their section of it, with the number of phantom units usually linked to salary. The value of the units increases by a predetermined amount as performance improves over a specified period; the formula may link the percentage increase in phantom units to the performance of the company's own non-ghostly stock. It's a good way of rubbing in the fact that the worker's fortunes are tied to those of the firm – and vice versa.

PIECEWORK – The oldest form of incentive payment and, once upon a time, the only way in which industrial workers got their money. Each piece of work carried a price in money wages: the more pieces, the more money. The piecework principle of "more for more" still underlies much more sophisticated, complex and often cumbersome modern forms of incentive pay. But straight piecework has gone out of the window, by and large, because the workers have no guarantee of a livelihood; management, by definition, can't reduce labour cost per unit of output – and may not even be able to raise output if the workers cut off at a given level of reward.

In fact, piecework deprives management of control over production and is totally unsuited to the age of automation. But wait – there's a growing, maybe swelling practice among even large companies of contracting-out work to people who operate from their homes. No work, no pay. More work, more pay. So old-fashioned, obsolete piecework is making a comeback – even if that's not what it's called.

PIGGYBACKING – In transportation, putting one load on top of another. In marketing, giving another firm's products a ride on top of your own distribution system. In theory, both sides benefit. The piggybacker gets a contribution from the piggybacked firm, which in turn doesn't have to pay the full cost of its distribution and marketing. On the other hand, it won't achieve the full sales potential, either.

PIMS – Profit impact of market strategy – a curious name for what is actually a database (*see* DBMS) covering a thousand different businesses and seeking to draw lessons from their comparative performance. The major conclusion drawn from PIMS (and explaining its curious name) was that the higher the market share, the higher the profitability – a finding highly consistent with those of the Boston Consulting Group (BCG).

Later studies have challenged the concept, largely on the clear ground that lower market share can equate with high profitability (if rarely), while high market share (quite commonly, in fact) doesn't necessarily equate with high returns on investment. If that was all that PIMS had to offer, it would be less important than it actually is – but the data throw up many other interesting considerations.

For example, it seems that you get a better return from top quality if your business lies in stagnant markets than if its markets are growing fast. Also, you get higher profitability from heavy spending on R&D if your product life-cycle has reached the stage of maturity than if it is still in the stage of relative growth. PIMS, in other words, provides plenty of food for thought, the essential nutrient of effective management. (*See also*: BCG; R&D; Product Life-Cycle.)

PLOUGHBACK – Funds earned by the company and neither paid to the tax man nor to the shareholders as dividends. Instead, they're ploughed back into investment in the firm. In theory, this enriches the shareholders more than if they had received the money in taxable dividends. In practice, that obviously depends on the directors earning more on the ploughed-back funds than the shareholders could have achieved elsewhere. All too often, the directors fail even this simple test. (*See also*: Retained Earnings.)

PLURAL EXECUTIVE – Vesting executive powers in more than one person. The "office of the chief executive" is the most common form of organisational pluralism – in addition to the chief executive, other executives (usually two or three) are associated with him at the head of the organisation. Supposedly, the chief executive in this set-up is only *primus inter pares*, the first among equals. In practice, he is usually so much more equal than the others that the plural executive, like the State in Marx's unfulfilled vision, simply withers away.

POINT SYSTEM – In this method of job evaluation, the personnel people define the job factors involved in each job; work out a rating scale for every factor – giving each of them points; add up all the points for all the factors in each job; and arrive at a points total that gives the evaluation, for what it's worth.

POP – Point of purchase – the sharp end, in fact the very end of the retail chain, where money changes hands for the goods. It's also the point where the shrewd and good merchandiser seeks to make maximum impact to keep the buyer and attract his or her attention to other products offered by the company. (*See also*: Merchandising.)

PORTFOLIO – More properly applied to holdings of shares and other investments, the phrase became transferred in the seventies to corporate strategic planning. The idea is to consider all of the businesses in a diversified corporation with no more passion than if they were a bundle of different shares. You sell the shares that aren't performing, and move to replace them with others that will perform better (you hope).

The concept of the manager as an investor has its uses – making him realise that money (other people's money at that) is truly invested in every business he operates, and that every business must earn its keep on investment criteria (ROCE/ROI). But there's a crucial difference: the investor in shares is essentially passive, making only three decisions – buy, sell or hold. In contrast, the manager takes an active role in the affairs of his "holdings" and makes many decisions, some of which may have profound effects on their value. The fact is that many businesses dropped as "dogs" under portfolio theory have shown much better performance on all counts in other, more effective, managerial hands. However, while the portfolio fashion has passed, its best feature has remained – which is the reminder to diversified managements that, with their strategic hat on, they must look at their business holdings as a whole – and must always be prepared to discard those that don't fit and to acquire new cards to strengthen the hand. (*See also*: Corporate Strategy; ROCE/ROI; PPM.)

POSDCORB – If you didn't know what a chief executive is supposed to do, you do now. This acronym was invented by Luther H. Gulick to describe precisely that: Planning, Organising, Staffing, Directing, Coordinating, Reporting and Budgeting. On the seventh day, the leader is allowed to rest. If he's lucky. (*See also*: CEO.)

POSITION – You position a product or service to place it, by a combination of price, attributes and availability, in the market segment from which you can achieve the best results. You also use positioning to differentiate your offerings from those of the opposition. Whether or not a company uses this concept consciously, everything it sells inevitably has a position. If the position is uncomfortable, you must move – and the sooner the better. (*See also*: Segmentation.)

POST AUDIT – Going back over the ground of a completed project to learn what lessons you can from the mistakes made, etc. Invaluable, and too rarely used.

PPBS – Planned programming budgeting system. This was hailed by many governments (including Britain's) as Washington's answer to the control of government spending. That it didn't work is manifest from the swelling of US deficits under president after president – but the idea's good for all that. The government department – or any other organisation – first sets out its objectives one by one and then treats as a group or as "programmes" all the activities that are concerned with meeting one of the objectives.

The budget is then tied to the programme, not to department or division, and financial and other controls (the review part of the exercise) are also applied specifically to the programme. In business, this approach is especially valuable for new ventures that need separating out – for that gives both better, proper control and better chances of success. But in government, PPBS foundered on the fact that programmes that overrun are no easier to control politically than departments that overspend – as British attempts to adopt the approach duly demonstrated.

PPM – Stands for "product portfolio management" – a method of looking at a diversified company's businesses to arrive at a strategy for maximising its results. The idea is that you examine, analyse and weigh the businesses like an investor looking at a portfolio of shares. But there's a big and vital difference: PPM uses a formal system to grade the items in the portfolio.

You draw a "matrix", usually consisting of nine squares, forming one large rectangle. On the left-hand side of the rectangle there's a scale of "market attractiveness" – low at the bottom, medium in the middle, high at the top. Along the bottom of the rectangle, the scale measures the corporate competitive strengths – low at the left, medium in the middle, high on the right. The PPM user has to decide where each business fits on both scales, so that he can derive the appropriate strategy.

For example, if the market is of medium attractiveness and the corporate strengths in that business are also middling, you choose what Kenichi Ohmae, author of *The Mind of the Strategist*, calls "selective expansion": meaning that you concentrate investment and expand only in segments where profitability is good and risk is relatively low. Altogether, Ohmae lists nine possible courses of action, starting with the worst situation (low attractiveness, low strength), where the policy is (1) *loss minimising* ("prevent losses before they occur by avoiding investment and by lowering fixed costs; when loss is unavoidable, withdraw"). Then, in ascending order, the strategies are: (2) *overall harvesting* ("promote switch from fixed to variable costs; emphasise profitability through value engineering and value analysis of variable costs"); (3) *limited harvesting* ("reduce degree of risk to a minimum in several segments; emphasise profit by protecting profitability even if loss of market position is involved"); (4) *limited expansion or withdrawal* ("look for ways of achieving expansion without high risk; if unsuccessful, withdraw before involved too deeply"); (5) *maintenance of superiority* ("build up ability to counter competition, avoiding large-scale investment; emphasise profitability by raising productivity"); (6) *selective expansion* (see above); (7) *serious entry into the market* ("opportunistic position to test growth prospects; withdraw if indications of sustainable growth are lacking"); (8) *selective growth* ("select areas where strength can be maintained, and concentrate investment in those areas"); (9) *all-out struggle* ("concentrate entire effort on maintaining strength; if necessary maintain profit structure by investment").

This approach has a close family resemblance to the Boston Consulting Group's famous four-square matrix, which classifies businesses as stars, question marks, cows (to be milked of their cash) and dogs (to be killed or sold). The idea is much less fashionable than it used to be, because (a) it's too mechanistic, and doesn't treat a business as a living organism; (b) it played into the hands of people who tried to manage conglomerates as purely financial operations; (c) it didn't work – the returns refused to be optimised.

The correct attitude? Use PPM as a tool to clarify your thoughts about a business. If your analysis puts it in a depressing part of the matrix, look again to see what can be done to shift it to a stronger square – not by playing around with PPM, but by positive, effective, dynamic management. (*See also*: Value Analysis; BCG.)

PREMIUM PRICING – Not only are some prices more attractive than others, even though they are higher, but some prices are more attractive than others *because* they are higher. This commonly applies to luxury or top-of-the-range items, whose high price is thought by the purchaser to be a guarantee of high quality.

Also, paying the high price adds to the prestige of the purchase and thus to that of the purchaser – which is why "prestige pricing" is sometimes used. The process isn't infinite, of course. Even Rolls-Royce had to cut its car prices in the United States (in 1982) because the price had run too far ahead of the prestige.

PREVENTATIVE MAINTENANCE – Maintaining plant, machinery and other equipment on a regular scheduled basis, instead of waiting until it goes wrong. The economies in time saved by knowing exactly when the machine will be "down", and probably for how long, are large enough in themselves. These savings are still further enhanced by the fact that the thing will break down far less often and less seriously.

PRICE FIXING – Getting together by competitors to agree, or fix, the prices they will charge the public, in order to protect profits, is highly effective. It's also highly illegal. An excellent method for executives who want to court legal retribution. Yet despite the risk, price fixing happens much more often than it should – which is not at all.

PRICE LEADER – A nice, legal way of price fixing is the old game of following the leader. The company with the largest market share in an industry with few competitors typically leads all price movements, both upwards (nearly always) and downwards (very seldom). The others then follow the lead at different, discreet, but very short intervals. Since the practice smacks of price fixing, the authorities are liable to get suspicious once in a while.

But it's not generally in the interests of the price followers, anyway. Loss of the competitive weapon of pricing simply removes part of the armoury with which they might attempt to oust, rather than follow, their leader. Also the *de facto* price ring is vulnerable to attacks from non-member outsiders. And that can inflict terrible pain on everybody.

PRICE POINT – Used in the strategy of marketing goods at predetermined prices, or producing and purchasing them so that they can be sold at such prices – known as price points and chosen by the vendor because he believes that his optimum sales will be achieved at the price concerned. The old Woolworths was a classic British example of the policy which in the US gave birth to the "Five and Tens", with their two price points of 5 and 10 cents. Michael Marks began Marks & Spencer's even more simply: "Don't Ask the Price, It's a Penny".

In modern conditions, selling to a price is a much more complex business: but you still see innumerable examples – including "price-lining" – where a company (say, a record manufacturer) will have only three price points (budget, mid-priced, and full-priced) even though the cost of production of different records at the same price varies greatly. The influence on the consumer of the actual price (quite apart from the value it represents) should never be ignored. (*See also*: Psychological Price.)

PRIME COST – When you're making something, the material, labour, and other expenses used directly in the manufacture of a unit of output are the prime cost. Combined with any other costs that vary with the number of units produced (but excluding fixed costs, which are the same whether you make one article or one hundred), prime cost gives you the marginal cost, i.e., the amount by which costs will rise if you raise production by one more unit. (*See also*: Marginal.)

PROBABILITY – Since all management deals with unpredictable events, the only way in which order can be brought to their prior assessment is by putting numbers to their likelihood. In certain low-level applications (like the number of defects that will occur from a machine's operation, or the number of sales a sales force will achieve in a given period), the calculations can be quite pretty and pretty useful.

The precondition is that you must know a number of possible outcomes to which you can then give "probabilities" – on a range between zero and one, with all the nine decimal points in between; the sum of all the probabilities must be one. In the low-level situations mentioned above, the probabilities are arrived at by experience, i.e., records of what's happened in the past.

To take the sales performance mentioned above, which target should management choose? The chances of the man coming back with no orders in a day, based on experience, are quite low (0.2); for just one the figure is 0.4; two orders comes up with a value of 0.3; and three is pretty unlikely – 0.1. If the firm is making a profit of £100 per unit sold, the expectation is £0 for 0, £40 for one, £60 for two, and £30 for three. This gives however, an average of £130 profit that the management can expect. However, following Bayes's rule it should strive with might and main to get sales up to two per salesman – that being the course with the highest expectation and the target on which the salesmen's commissions should be based.

In higher-level applications, the judgments are subjective. The manager must decide, on the basis of knowledge and available data, how probable or improbable an outcome is. The technique is an invaluable and often stupidly overlooked method of thinking cleverly in an organised way. (*See also*: Bayesian Theory; Decision Theory.)

PRODUCT – Used to mean a manufactured object. But the emphasis has now moved away sharply from making to selling. A product is now, in management parlance, anything that is offered for sale to the public. Thus, a magazine (which is partly manufactured) is now a product; but so is a financial service, like some variety of insurance policy, which isn't manufactured at all.

The point (and it's a valuable one) of the borrowed nomenclature is to emphasise the basic principle of market orientation. Neither the manufactured object nor the available service has any value until purchased by the customer. The latter in turn isn't buying the thing, but the bundle of attributes and (he hopes) satisfactions that go with it. What defines a product, then, is the value as perceived by the customer – quite right, too.

PRODUCT CONTROL – The system of operating periodic review of a company's products to ensure that those which need improvement or change to meet marketing or profitability objectives are changed, and that those which cannot meet those goals are eliminated. Control can be exercised on a formal basis, using a rating system. Whether formal or informal, though, the process of cutting out the weak and strengthening the strong is the essence of successful product strategy in any firm. (*See also*: Rating Scale.)

PRODUCTION CYCLE – The whole gamut of operations from receipt of an order to dispatch of the finished article or articles. The length of the cycle is traditionally much longer than the time actually taken to make the object – often by a factor of 10 to 1. The extra time (which costs much money) is taken up in queuing before production even starts; between all stages as bottlenecks develop and transfer takes too long; and finally in store before shipment takes place.

These awful diseconomies were taken for granted in Western companies (most of which didn't even bother to calculate the time lost) until the Japanese showed that better organisation of methods could bring actual cycle times and theoretical ones very close together. In some cases, 20-day cycles have come down to 20 hours, with total elimination of buffer stocks between processes, great speeding-up of delivery times, and vast benefits to the firm's cash flow. (*See also*: Queuing Theory; Cash Flow.)

PRODUCTION MANAGEMENT – Formerly the Cinderella, now not quite the princess of management specialities. In the days when Cinderella slaved away in the kitchen, her sisters (ugly or not) in marketing, finance, or general management stood in the limelight – and held all the top jobs. It took the rise of the Japanese and the decline in Western productivity to demonstrate what should always have been obvious: that a manufacturing company rests on the efficiency of its manufacturing operation.

In consequence, production management has shot up in status and pay – rightly, for there's no task in management more demanding than planning, operating, and renewing the production process: juggling with capacity and capability to produce at the lowest possible cost the required volumes with the desired levels of quality. Without these, the marketing men are helpless and the figures produced by finance will be hopeless.

PRODUCTIVITY – Simple to define, but harder to apply, productivity measures output in relation to input. Thus, if the output of a plant is £1 million during a period when 100,000 man-hours are supplied, output per man-hour is £10. Compare that to the previous similar period, when the figure was 8, and you've got a 25% increase in the productivity of labour.

That's the easy bit. The tough part comes in deciding what generated the higher productivity. If management has installed faster-running machines, say, or if the product mix has shifted toward costlier machines because of consumer demand, there's been no real gain. It wouldn't make too much sense, then, to raise wages because of the higher productivity of labour. The same kind of objection may apply if the output is measured in physical units as opposed to hard cash.

Other inputs can be related to output in the same way: for instance, the productivity of capital (how much output per pound of capital invested) is a number that has given some horrendous results in recent years – a good reason, no doubt, why most managements failed to use it. For all its imperfections, measurement of productivity trends is fundamentally important to their improvement – and that is fundamentally important to any operation.

PRODUCTIVITY BARGAINING – The idea of trading wage increases for improved working practices that will raise productivity sounds fine. Looked at more closely, it enshrines two serious defects. First, the work force is being given the option to continue with inefficient practices – where management's job is to eliminate them. Second, the payment (or bribe) is guaranteed, while the productivity benefits are not. Managements that get involved in this often tortuous process are really bargaining not about productivity, but about the right to manage – which they are abdicating.

PRODUCT LIFE-CYCLE – All products, in theory, go through a life-cycle whose four stages correspond to the seven-age progression of man from birth and growth to senescence and death. The First Age of products is "introduction", when sales are building up from a low level but prices are high – meaning that after break-even has been passed, the profit contribution per unit (marginal profit) will be very high, too.

The Second Age is that of "growth". Sales are rising rapidly, and unit profits are at their maximum until the Third Age, that of "maturity"; sales level off, competition increases, prices come under pressure and profitability starts to fall.

Sooner or later, the Fourth Age, that of decline, comes about. Sales start to fall, prices and the profits dribble away, and eventually the product gets killed.

Note the verb "gets killed". Occasionally a product may really die – that is, nobody's buying the offending object any more. But usually some management decides that enough is enough and wields the axe. Quite often, it does so wrongly: a lively product is being killed. Seeing that the product is "mature", management withholds financial and other support or milks it as a "cash cow".

That decision is a self-fulfilling prophecy. Because of the lack of support, the product proceeds, usually at some speed, from maturity to decline. While the changing from growth to maturity is inevitable, determined by markets rather than management, growth can be sustained and maturity made more profitable by brand renewal and product extension, using features and variants to create new market segments and new customers in old segments.

A classic example is the way in which Japanese manufacturers have successfully kept sales of quality cameras moving by a series of innovations that have maintained interest in the single-lens reflex product – while adding new sales through all-automatic compact 35mm cameras, some of them more costly than SLRs. In many other cases (think only of corn flakes and detergents), the product life-cycle is still showing no sign of decline after many decades.

But the last couple of decades have seen an outburst of new exceptions – products where the Four Ages are determined not by the market, but by technology. If you're making 16k RAM (Random Access Memory) microcircuits when 32k RAMs hit the market, or 32ks when 64s arrive, or 64s when 256s take over, no power on earth will stop growth becoming maturity becoming decline. The phenomenon has passed over into electronic consumer goods – and it's a whole new world for the product life-cycle and its protagonists. (*See also*: Cash Cow; Segmentation; Product Line.)

PRODUCT LINE – The range of products offered by a company – often used in the narrow sense of a group of related products, as in a line of cameras. A variant is the same product with a difference – strawberry flavour, or a convertible version of a car, or (to cite cameras again) a model with autofocus. An extension is the addition of a new model or models serving the same market – say, a compact camera added to a range of single-lens reflex models – but generally seeking to appeal to new buyers.

The tendency is for product lines to proliferate with variants, extensions, etc., until one day the company engages in product line rationalisation or pruning, to eliminate the weak sellers, reduce costs across the whole line, and concentrate attention on the best selling and most profitable products. The results are invariably most gratifying. (*See also*: Rationalisation.)

PRODUCT MANAGER – The executive placed in charge of a particular product and held responsible for its performance in the marketplace. In fast-moving consumer goods (FMCG) the more likely name is brand manager. The responsibility has often been more theoretical than real, since nobody's going to leave somebody (especially somebody young) in sole, undisputed charge of a brand on which a major chunk of the corporate fortunes depend.

In some companies, though, the logic of product management has been followed right through the firm. Here the product manager starts his responsibility at the beginning of the development process and stays with the product into production and market introduction.

The manager also oversees the further developments of the product, and has a global responsibility for its market performance. Product managers may be given more than one product to look after, too, which is one clear indication that the role has more to do with coordination than true masterminding. Even so, it's not true that the more the merrier. Concentrated and genuinely responsible product management is an excellent way of developing both the manager and the business. (*See also*: FMCG.)

PRODUCT MIX – Few things are more important in determining profit than the mix of products – how much of each kind of product a company makes and markets. The more a company makes of items with high added value and the less of low, the more profitable it will be.

Sadly, the market will never allow the company to mix its products in exactly the most profitable proportions. But it's still vitally important to know exactly what contribution each component of the mix produces; without that information it's impossible to construct a sensible manufacturing and marketing strategy – or to take action that will increase the contribution of the lower added-value lines.

That's greatly helped by product line rationalisation. The rational management seeks to reduce the number of lines in the mix, cutting out those that are too small or contribute too little to justify their retention, and using design engineering to maximise the number of common parts and processes in the lines retained. The firm that doesn't seek to maximise the mix in this way has only itself to blame for its mixed results. (*See also*: Added Value; Contribution; Rationalisation.)

PROFIT – Whether you call the number profit, earnings, or income, it's the prime objective of business – to receive more in revenues than it pays out in expenses. The definition sounds entirely simple, but applying it actually involves more difficulty than using added value. That's because both of the elements of profit (revenues and expenses) are subject to different interpretations, while the fact that business finances involve capital costs as well as current ones must also be taken into account.

Further, the profit figure is the one on which taxation is based – which gives sensible managements the incentive to minimise rather than maximise profits. A welter of different considerations and conventions means that comparisons of different corporate profits are often misleading – while the trouble is much worse across frontiers, since national practices (even by honest companies) differ so markedly.

What can be said with total clarity, though, is that each firm does make a true profit or loss – that is, the business is worth more (or less) at the end of one financial period than it was at the beginning. It's also incontrovertibly true that the business which doesn't make adequate and rising profits in reality (never mind what it shows on paper) won't make it in the long run – and maybe not in the short, either. (*See also*: Added Value.)

PROFIT CENTRE – A discrete part of a company charged with producing a separately indentifiable profit. The concept of the profit centre was basic to the decentralisation drive in corporations and to the philosophy of identifying and increasing management responsibility down the line. It's not enough just to isolate part of the business and make its management responsible for hitting its own individual profit target – that's unrealistic unless the management has the required resources and control over its destiny.

Failure to provide these necessities partly explains the innumerable failures of the profit-centre principle to guarantee the profit growth that the targets implied. But as an organisational device, the profit centre has greatly improved control and visibility – especially since managements have realised that many activities are cost centres rather than profit ones, and need managing accordingly. (*See also*: Cost Centre).

PROJECT MANAGEMENT – As the size, cost and complexity of projects has increased, so has the awareness that their management requires special skills and separation from other corporate activities. Above all, it demands placing one project manager in charge. Presumably, that's what happened with the nuclear power stations that overran their costs by ten times. Which proves that sensible techniques don't always have sensible results.

PSC – On the face of it, process statistical control is just another name for SQC (statistical quality control). But it's not merely a question of a rose by any other name … although the name matters. Where SQC might seem like something you leave to the lower, technical echelons of management, PSC has been sold to top management – and its key principles have been taught to many senior people in the renewed drive for higher quality.

Also, "process" rubs in the vital point that quality doesn't begin and end with the product, but is the result of the entire production operation: that, to build on the basic perception that you can't inspect quality into a product, management must have a comprehensive system running all the way from design to delivery. Also, PSC clearly must involve the supplier as well, so the statistical sampling method is used to "rate" suppliers, who won't keep the business unless they get a "top supplier" rating.

That means that their own processes, too, must be under control. The requirements are: (1) measurements; (2) coupling these to basic statistical laws to get viable information on what's actually happening in the process – because you can't control what you can't measure; (3) computing – thanks to the microprocessor, you can use PSC without swamping the whole outfit in paperwork.

The results should include: (1) working to proper specifications instead of unrealistically tight tolerances – often chosen by engineering because it feels that production won't conform (with PSC, so-called "statistical tolerancing" gives everybody more elbow room), (2) an opportunity to enhance employee participation, because PSC involves the workers in some of its key procedures (like measurement), and provides a powerful medium for their training sessions – and, more important, imbues them with the whole philosophy of doing things right, and doing them right first time. In one car plant, for instance, a major element in improving productivity and quality alike was a piece of expensive equipment issued to every man: a 6-inch ruler. (*See also*: SQC.)

PSYCHOLOGICAL PRICE – Sounds like the cost of seeing a psychiatrist, but actually refers to the fact that some prices ("charm prices", as they are called) are more attractive to customers than others – and not necessarily because they are cheaper. Thus 99 pence has greater "charm" than £1 – but also more than 96 pence. Charm prices are usually the "price points" at which marketers aim. (*See also*: Price Point.)

PTMS – Predetermined time-motion system. Times for basic elements of human movement are used as building blocks to establish how long the task being analysed should take. PTMS saves a lot of time – as a method and in its results.

PURCHASES-TO-SALES RATIO – The proportion of a company's sales that is accounted for by its purchases from outside the company. The ratio is a measure of the degree or otherwise of vertical integration. Customarily, the higher the market share, the lower the purchases-to-sales ratio. However, the custom may be changing, for in many industries that are now among the fastest growing (especially electronics), even the largest competitors in terms of market share are now buying heavily from outside suppliers – in some cases purchasing not merely components, but whole assemblies. (*See also*: Vertical Integration.)

Q

QC – For one brief, heady moment, quality circles were hailed as the secret of Japanese managements. If that had only been true . . . all Western firms would have needed to do was to introduce the circles, and the Japanese would have been defeated with their own weapons. Many Westerners did, in fact, jump on to the QC bandwagon. And even though QCs have turned out to be only a minor contributor to Japanese achievements, the QCs have demonstrated that, in the right hands and used in the right way, they can work anywhere.

The basic definition, as given by David Hutchins, is that a group "of workers from a shop or department meet regularly under the leadership of a foreman or section head to examine work problems that affect the quality of output, and to recommend solutions to these problems". The number of workers is usually six to eight, and membership is absolutely voluntary – meaning that in a Japanese company, *everybody* belongs.

As that indicates, the QCs are not stand-alone devices in the land of their fathers, but one manifestation of a whole philosophy of work and management. They can work all on their own; they work much better in the context of a programme for participation or quality of working life (QWL).

Either way, success of the actual circle obviously depends on the contribution that can be made by solving the particular problem. Give the circle an insignificant problem and you'll get an insignificant result. QCs thus need a Pareto analysis before they start – to ensure that they only concern themselves with the 20% of the section's work that gives rise to 80% of the costs or the quality problems.

Actually attacking a quality problem requires detailed work and technical know-how: the mastery, for instance, of a fishbone diagram. It sets out to draw all possible causes and (maybe) sub-causes of a defined quality failure on a "cause and effect" diagram – "effect" here meaning the occurrence of a quality lapse. Because of the need for technical know-how, training, and coordination across departments, a QC programme needs someone called a facilitator, who knows the ropes and the company.

Proponents of QCs are fairly fanatical about them, and will tell you that a return on the investment of between 5–1 and 8–1 is generally achieved. Critics say that, once you've shared any supposed savings with the QC members (which is essential), the company may really be in the red on the deal. Which only rubs in the main point: don't let the circles stand alone. (*See also*: QWL; Pareto's Law.)

QCIP – Quality cost improvement plans – an approach originally developed at ITT by Philip Crosby, author of *Quality Is Free* and *Quality Without Tears*. The programme was credited with saving ITT the equivalent of 5% of sales income not only by eliminating waste (defined as the costs of failure), but also by cutting down the heavy costs of monitoring operations through inspection and testing, etc.

The QCIP approach rests on the ancient principle that prevention is better than cure. To achieve the best results, a QCIP must work hand in hand with efficient design, work planning, supplier surveillance, operative training, etc. But the QCIP has a role all its own – starting with the identification by detailed study of all significant areas where money is being wasted (obvious targets are scrap, rectification of defects, re-work).

Crosby's full treatment has fourteen steps. But the principles can be covered more briefly as follows. Study of where excess costs are being incurred is followed up by identification of the actual costs (establishing a benchmark for the improvements to be made). The items are then listed in descending order of cost – and the top half-dozen most costly, or some other number, are selected for urgent attention. The remedies emerge from group work involving every department concerned. The important point is to agree clearly on the corrective action, and to decide without any shadow of a doubt that it will be taken.

Next, it is taken. The progress of the plans is monitored until the point when the target cost savings have been achieved. Then the QCIP moves on to the next items down the list of cost rankings – and the process continues until the overall target has been achieved.

Ideally, you don't stop until savings reach that 5% of sales income. And you don't stop there, either. While experience shows that you won't get any further improvement beyond the 5%, if you don't keep the QCIP going, one thing's for sure. The waste will come creeping back.

QUEUING THEORY – Every business operation involves queues, or the possibility of queues; if it isn't people waiting in line to be served, or to pay, it's semi-finished products waiting for the next stage of processing. The same mathematical theory governs all such situations and is used to reduce the length of the queue without a wasteful increase in the resources used.

Waste would arise if, say, you doubled the number of super-market checkouts, greatly cutting down the time people spend in line, but at huge extra cost during the periods when there wouldn't be queues in any event. The "theory of queues", or "waiting-line theory", enables the management scientist to anal-yse the queue, predict how long people will spend in it, and recommend action to minimise the queues and the time. If only more managements would use it . . .

QWL – American industry's answer to the Japanese challenge has included, in quality of working life programmes, an effort to match the integration of Japanese workers with the management and ethos of the company. QWL programmes contain a good measure of job enrichment and enlargement. But their main contribution so far in companies like General Motors has been, for the first time, to involve workers, supervisors, and management in finding ways of improving performance and getting greater working harmony. It's strange that what is basically common sense – that the more people are involved and interested in their work, the better they will do it – needed a new acronym and new programmes to be recognised. But better late than never. (*See also*: Job Enrichment.)

R

RATING SCALE – If you're comparing two rival investment projects, you could say that X is preferable to Y because it offers a higher return on capital (ROCE), but that Y offers a higher growth potential. You could go on to say that growth matters more to you than return. But that doesn't answer the essential question – how much more?

The rating scale technique ascribes numerical values to the preferences; put another way, it seeks to translate qualitative judgments into quantities. That not only enables comparisons to be made more easily; it forces the judge to be stricter about his judgments.

The simplest approach is the old one-two, or, to be precise, the 0–1–2, where 0 = bad, 1 = average, and 2 = good. If you use "interval measurement", you're treating the difference between two ratings, using bigger numbers on a scale to 100, as significant – that is, a gap of 10 means that you think the difference between the two qualities is twice as important as where the difference is only 5.

Or you could use percentages – a "ratio scale" – in which the intervals are calculated by reference to a base, customarily zero, where whatever quality you're comparing doesn't exist at all. The precise method used is less important than the principle of making subjective assessments as objective as you possibly can – while remembering that they're still subjective. (*See also*: ROCE/ROI.)

RATIO – The relationship by simple division of one number (say, profits) to another (say, capital employed) is the fundamental tool of business analysis. The ratio just mentioned (ROCE) is a financial one, but the tool can be applied anywhere in the business: number of machine hours used can be divided by total machine hours available, successful calls by salesman can be divided by total calls, and so on.

Not only are these ratios (commonly expressed as percentages) a quick and clear guide to performance internally, but when used by like companies they provide the material for inter-firm comparisons. That way, management can highlight its low spots in performance terms. What gives ratios their power is the reverse of what makes single numbers useless – that unless you can relate them to other relevant statistics, you know nothing about the dynamics of the business or its real performance. (*See also*: ROCE/ROI; Inter-firm Comparison.)

RATIONALISATION – The reduction or rearrangement of assets and labour employed so as to perform the corporate task more effectively. The word is something of a euphemism, used because it sounds better to rationalise a plant than to shut it down at the cost of several thousand jobs. Still, it truly is irrational to keep an operation going that can't make anything save losses and is performing no useful economic function – and the job of management is to apply rational principles and thought to rationally presented problems.

It isn't only facilities that may need rationalisation; product lines have increasingly received the rational treatment, with low-selling products dropped, and others redesigned to make greater use of commonality of parts. Distribution networks, too, nearly always throw up excessive costs that can be eliminated by rationalisation – concentrating on fewer warehouses, or eliminating uneconomic customers whose orders are too small or too costly to service.

While, as noted, rationalisation is basic to the business of effective management, it's usually true that, where massive rationalisation becomes necessary, somebody has mismanaged in the past – usually many somebodies over far too much of the past. Continuous rationalisation is the answer: it shouldn't hurt at all, though discontinuous rationalisation can hurt terribly. (*See also*: Product Line; Commonality.)

R&D – The key to a corporation's future revenue is its investment in future products – and increasingly these rest to some extent on *R* (for research) and a great deal on *D* (for development). In point of fact, few corporations do much in the way of original research – that is, developing scientific knowledge that is not known anywhere else. Where corporations have contributed to genuine theoretical advance, there's often a clear split between the *R* and the *D* – as at AT&T, whose Bell Labs came up with brilliant *R* breakthroughs like the transistor. But their exploitation, or *D*, was the business of the manufacturing arm, Western Electric. The *R* function has most importance, and attracts most financial support, self-evidently, wherever the future depends most heavily on new inventions – as in the pharmaceutical companies, which have in fact accounted for a large number of fundamental discoveries down the years.

Even where the R&D is all *D*, though, the management dimension poses real difficulties – how much money to allocate, what time-spans to expect, when to cut away if no results come forth. The company has to strike a balance between running R&D like any other business, in which case the scientists and engineers are unlikely to produce any wonders, or running R&D like a university lab, in which case the wonders may not be economic or economically discovered.

Whichever solution or approach is adopted, two things are sure: (a) you can't do it on the cheap, (b) the price of staying in the race is rising all the time – and a high ratio of R&D expenditure to sales has become one of the most vital indicators of good corporate health.

REAL TIME – What used to be a rarity in EDP (electronic data processing) has become a commonplace. From airline reservation systems to supermarket checkouts, the information supplied is processed at once and becomes immediately available to any user of the system. That's the talent which has progressed the computer from bookkeeping into the heart of real, real-time management.

RED-LINING – If the company won't do business in a certain area – for example, if it won't give consumer credit to families living in a poor district – there's an imaginary red line (and maybe not an imaginary one) drawn round the offending district. Red-lining has now become global – there are less-developed countries (LDCs) which, you can be sure, have certainly been red-lined by the world's commercial banks – whether they admit it or not. (*See also*: LDC.)

REGRESSION ANALYSIS – An indispensable statistical technique, if you want (as you often do in market research) to infer the relationship between two sets of figures. If there are only two, there's a "simple regression analysis" to perform. More likely than not, there will be several so-called "independent variables" as well as the control "dependent variable"; in that case, you've got a "multiple regression analysis" on your hands. (*See also*: Market Research.)

REMUNERATION – Pay – primarily executive pay. Strangely, in the US the word compensation, with its roots in making financial restitution to somebody and assuaging some loss that he's suffered, has been commonly adopted for this purpose. "Remuneration", "emoluments", or just straight "pay" sound much more straightforward. The American loss, presumably, that's being compensated for is that of time and effort expended in the job – but that's a very odd concept of the relationship between the executive and his employer.

The other words, note, are all more direct about the fact that money changes hands. So maybe compensation comes in handy to cover – or semantically conceal – the fact that US "compensation programmes" or "packages" only contain an element of straight pay, which is added to by fringe benefits, and may be heavily outweighed by incentive bonuses and, above all, by share options.

This element isn't supposed to be straight pay, and isn't treated as such by the tax authorities. But of course it's just as much a transfer of value from the corporation to the manager as a bonus or even his simple pay packet. (*See also*: Share Option.)

RETAINED EARNINGS – Profit that isn't paid out to the shareholders in dividends (or to anybody else as interest or whatever) ends up as the "undistributed profits" or "retentions" or "earned surplus" or retained earnings. They are what enable the directors to "plough back" money into developing and expanding the business. Evidently, this is the lifeblood of the future, and high retentions have usually been associated in people's minds with dynamism and high growth.

It won't work out that way, though, unless the firm is making a sufficient return on investment (or ROI) on the capital concerned; and it won't really work out for the shareholders unless the retentions (which actually belong to them) are being invested at a higher return than they can earn for themselves. But the amount of ploughback has seldom been questioned – partly because the tax laws in most lands favour the investment of money before it reaches the shareholders' hands.

Peter Drucker has been foremost in attacking the fiscal system for the distortion that this produces – leaving too much capital in the hands of fat, established companies, which, by definition, won't use it as dynamically and profitably as new and hungry managements. (*See also*: ROCE/ROI; Ploughback.)

RIGHT FIRST TIME – Just what it says – a programme for improving corporate and individual performance by exhorting and training people to accomplish their tasks precisely and invariably. They won't, of course, but the effort to do so will raise both performance and morale.

RINGI – *Ringiseido* means in Japanese "a system of reverential inquiry about a superior's intentions". Abbreviated to *ringi*, it has come to mean, in the West, consensus decision making, Japanese style. But there's more to it than that in Japan. Say there's a problem. The subordinate manager who is faced with it, and has worked out a solution, asks his section chief to call a meeting on the subject.

If the meeting decides that the idea has merit, but requires higher and broader support, the department head is approached. If he approves, the *ringi* process starts. All the departments involved could be asked to a meeting (meaning sixteen to twenty people, including any staff experts required). If the discussion throws up a need for more input, the manager who first had the brainwave goes round collecting all the extra information and whatever else is required.

The process of discussion and collection goes on until the original department head reckons that enough is really enough. Then *nemawashi* (the real word for decision making by consensus) ends, and the *ringi* part – getting authorisation – begins: the original deep management thinker and others, supervised by the section head, write up the *ringi-sho*. This is a formal document, supported by the relevant information and so forth. And it's this *sho* (*sho* means document) that goes right up the management structure, receiving seals of approval from those who approve.

By the time the very summit of the corporation receives the *sho*, it may have as many as a dozen seals; then it's ready for the ultimate authorisation by top management – which may, in fact, have originally presented the problem for solution, but which wouldn't dream of handing down an imposed solution from on high.

In theory, the system is very long-winded. In practice, it's a laborious, but ultimately effective way, not only of testing a solution to destruct, but of obtaining commitment to the solution by everybody affected – because they've all been involved with the decision-making process all along the line.

RISK MANAGEMENT – In a corporate world where the risks are legion, and wildly unpredictable, the risk manager seeks to reduce the corporation's exposure by all possible means. He has three possible weapons, of which the most important is prevention: wherever action can be taken to forestall danger – by tightening up security, fitting roof sprinklers to combat fire, or whatever – it's taken. But accidents will still happen, and the company can cover itself against these by self-insurance, putting money aside to cover the risks; or by external insurance, paying an outside insurer. Many companies make the latter an automatic and exclusive choice. It's an expensive option, though.

It's also true, of course, that nobody can forestall, or even foresee, all risks. Johnson & Johnson had no means of knowing that a homicidal maniac would tamper with paracetamol capsules on sale. Had it known, the preventative measures taken afterwards (the tamper-proof packs) would have been taken beforehand. Which is the whole point of risk management.

ROBOTICS – Purists are getting very pernickety about the proper use of the word robot. Most of the robots currently in use do one operation over and over again, substituting for human operatives in repetitive and/or dangerous jobs which the humans are only too glad to hand over. These robots aren't really different in principle from numerically controlled machine tools – the difference lies only in the direct substitution of a metal hand for a human one.

The true robot, however, is the product of cybernetics. To quote one writer, "True robots are programmable manipulating machines which are capable of operating in stand-alone applications, in conjunction with human skills or together with other flexible manufacturing equipment." The advanced robot can perform several tasks, and can modify how and when it does them, using electronic sensors to replace human senses of touch, sight, etc., and both getting orders and giving feedback through a computer.

In the FMC, or factory of the future, for which robotics are essential, the whole plant in a sense becomes a giant robot, performing its task without human intervention, while responding constantly to changing information about the process. Just like a human, in fact – except that the robot reacts faster – and doesn't argue.

ROCE/ROI – Return on capital employed, or return on invest-ment, went abruptly out of fashion as a corporate measure, but came back equally fast when companies realised the dreadful consequences of letting ROCE fall below the cost of equity. That can happen – with the inevitable consequence of a fall in the price of the shares – even though once more fashionable objectives, like a target rise in earnings per share, are indeed being met. There are many theoretical objections to ROCE (usually the profit after tax divided by the capital employed), mainly the questions of what accounting principles have been used in working out the profit – and whether the capital employed is a meaningful figure.

But the objections apply mainly to comparing one firm's ROCE with another. Assuming consistent treatment between years, the ROCE figure is an indispensable guide to year-to-year perform-ance of companies in nearly all industries. Apart from anything else, ROCE also measures how well/badly the company is using its resources by comparison with returns on capital available in financial markets. Within the firm, too, it provides an essential yardstick for comparing divisions and investment projects. Don't let anybody knock ROCE in general or defend a low one in particular. It's indefensible. (*See also*: Cost of Equity; Earnings Yield; Capital; Profit.)

ROLE PLAYING – A much-favoured form of training. The stu-dents are asked to take on different parts in a situation that mimics real life – the salesman trying to close a sale with a difficult prospect, a superior conducting a dismissal interview with a difficult subordinate, and so on. In role reversal, the two players change parts. In role rotation, all the people involved in the training session take all the roles in turn.

The method has limitations – obviously real life inconveniently never imitates amateur dramatics. But putting yourself in some-body else's shoes is always valuable, and something useful always does rub off into the real-life activity. Also, it's important to recognise that managers do inevitably play different roles in different situations – and that the roles (critic, leader, facilitator, etc.) are all indispensable to an effective outcome.

ROS – Return on sales – the percentage obtained by dividing profit by the sales total – is easing into the limelight after the discovery that it's the key number used by Japanese companies. That's because, using so much low-cost bank finance, they have less need to concern themselves with ROCE. Instead they concentrate on profit divided by sales, and strive with might and main to maximise the figure.

The difference is more apparent than real, since the Japanese are also (rightly) insistent on a fast turnover of capital. If you're earning a high margin on sales, and achieving a high rate of sales in relation to capital, you must have a high ROCE. But the corollary is that a low ROS is a real sign of danger. That kind of number proves that there's something wrong with either the prices, the costs, the products, or the markets – very probably, all four combined. (*See also*: ROCE/ROI.)

RUCKER PLAN – Quite similar to the Scanlon Plan, another method for relating pay to improvements in labour productivity. Under the scheme designed by Allen W. Rucker, the incentive payment is spread across the entire plant. The key improvement watched for in the Rucker approach is that of the ratio of labour cost to added value – a ratio that really is one of the fundamentals in the health of any business.

The Rucker Plan includes joint committees, composed of management and worker representatives, and going under the name of "share-of-production committees". Their purpose is to look into ideas for improving operating efficiency. Their spiritual relationship to quality circles (QCs) and other Japanese methods is evident, but the Rucker stress on the spirit of cooperation and mutual dependence isn't anything like so clear. Productivity plans such as Rucker's and Scanlon's have always had to be sold to workers merely and mainly as a means of raising pay – and that is their gravest defect. (*See also*: Scanlon Plan; Added Value; QCs.)

S

SAFETY STOCK – Known by many other names, of which "buffer stock" is the most common. By these or any other names it has come to smell less sweet. If it's necessary to hold stock as a safety measure, or as a buffer, in case (a) the supplies don't turn up or (b) consumption of the item involved is higher than expected, then (by today's standards) the company is badly managed.

SALE AND LEASEBACK – If you own a property in which you're selling shoes – or making them, for that matter – a large amount of capital value is locked up in that property. You can release, or liberate, the capital by selling the property under an agreement by which you promptly lease it back.

It sounds wonderfully like having your cake and eating it – but you can't, of course. The notional cost of using the property when you owned it (which is the price at which it could have been rented out) becomes a real cost – and the profits will be reduced by that amount. You won't end up as a loser unless the rental on the leaseback is greater than the profits on the business being conducted in the premises – but if that's the case, you shouldn't be in business anyway.

SAMPLE – The basic tool of statistical analysis. The essence of the technique is the mathematical fact that a tiny part, a sample, of any group – up to a whole electorate – will provide all the information required to give a very nearly accurate picture of the totality:

hence political opinion polls. At the humdrum level of industrial life, sampling is fundamental to SQC (statistical quality control) and to much other essential activity like market research. Managers find it hard to believe that sampling in the factory yields better results, more cheaply, than 100% inspection. It does. (*See also*: SQC.)

SATISFICING – Managers tend to opt for playing it safe – taking the line of least resistance, or the "good enough" alternative – when they don't have enough time, enough information, enough analysis, enough clarity of goals – in other words, most of the time in most companies. Also, there's a natural tendency in all people to avoid risks, which reinforces what Nobel Prize winner Herbert A. Simon christened as "satisficing".

Since "good enough" may well not be good enough, the problem is plainly to ensure that you don't have the conditions which produce "satisficing", and which are themselves known as "bounded rationality". Provide better information, allow adequate time, make sure that thorough analysis has been done, and that people have clear goals – then rationality won't be bounded, and neither will the company's results.

SBU/SPU – "Strategic business units" are made up of "strategic planning units". The difference? A single product category would form an SPU – say, wine. If the company had no other products that fitted into the same business, that's as far as the SPU would go. But if it also handled spirits, the wine might well join the hard stuff in an alcoholic beverage SBU.

What for? The ruling philosophy, largely pioneered by General Electric, is that a division or a free-standing business should be organised around its market. If there's a shared logic (of distribution, promotion, production, technology, etc.), a strong case exists for joining like SPUs and getting the benefits of economies of scale (in R&D, or sales force, or production runs, etc.) in an SBU. That's not all, though. Below the SPU are its components: the PMS (product market segments), defined as the smallest units that can engage in competition. And above the SBU, there's the

SS – the strategic sector. And above that is the ultimate source of strategic power, at corporate headquarters.

This modish layout is designed to bind the whole company and its strategy together via a series of hierarchical stages. The successive strategic steps all exist somewhere in any company (setting the corporate goals, planning for the long term, strategy for the short and middle term, nuts-and-bolts planning at the business level, and the sharp end itself where the product meets the market – the PMS). The approach is designed to clarify where each purpose is located – and in doing so makes two emphases that are much more important than the hierarchic idea itself.

These ideas are *separation* and *likeness*. You *separate* a business so that its performance and purpose are perfectly clear, and so that a single management can be made clearly responsible for both. You join together *like* businesses so that the whole can be stronger than its parts. Either way, what you're trying to identify and plan is a *business*: a unit that makes cohesive sense to those who run it, and in the markets where it competes. That principle applies even if the company isn't some globe-girdling conglomerate but a small company where PMS, SPU, SBU, SS and HQ are one and the same thing.

SCANLON PLAN – Bears a close relation to quality circles in some respects, but the incentive payments loom much larger in an approach that long anticipated the US enthusiasm for QCs and similar Japanese methods. Joseph N. Scanlon, the inventor, was a trade union official (oddly enough) who died in 1956 – when practically nobody in the United States had heard of a Japanese car, still less thought of driving one.

Scanlon's approach was based on measuring the work done by every producing unit in the plant. One method was to find out what proportion of the value of output was represented by labour costs. The standard ratio was then compared to the actual. If the work force had bettered the standard, then the savings were shared between the company and the workers in a predetermined proportion.

That's not all, by any means. The plan includes joint management-worker committees that look at ways of saving costs from which further gains in productivity can be obtained. While some corporations have used the Scanlon Plan to notable effect, neither half of its pincer movement (the incentives nor the participative management) caught on fast enough in the United States to prevent the productivity gap widening as the Japanese advanced on this front.

Now more up-to-date motivational and participative techniques are being rushed into action in many companies in an effort to close the gap. But since the emphasis in raising productivity has moved from worker motivation to effective automation, the incentive payments that are fundamental to the Scanlon Plan have come to seem less attractive.

In some plants (like the Apple factory churning out Macintosh computers as fast as the traffic will bear), the labour costs are so tiny a proportion (1%) that no higher productivity worth having can be achieved on the manpower front. And machines don't respond to incentives at all. (*See also*: QC; Automation.)

SCENARIO PLANNING – Planning on the basis, not of one central forecast, but on a range of possible future outcomes. It arose because forecasters can only foretell the future correctly by accident – and the odds against their getting it right get worse and worse the further ahead they look. That being so, companies that have learned their forecasting the hard way now prefer to look at a range of possibilities. Usually their planners draw up three scenarios, which are all logically possible – given certain alternative assumptions.

For example, you could forecast oil prices on the basis of war in the Middle East, or on the usual uneasy, conflict-dotted stalemate, or on peace. Of course, you'd have to couple these alternatives with assumptions about Western economic growth. But the general pattern will still emerge as a worst case (Scenario A, say), a best case (Scenario C), and an in-between (Scenario B).

The manager's responsibility is then to weigh his responses in each of the three eventualities. Scenario planning thus shifts the onus from the planner getting it right (impossible) to the manager doing it right (very possible) – which, of course, is where the onus should always be. The manager is forced to ask the key question, "What if?" Even in its least sophisticated form (Best World, Worst World), the scenario approach still serves the invaluable purpose of making managers plan for eventualities – as opposed to being overtaken by them. (*See also*: Best World, Worst World.)

SCIENTIFIC MANAGEMENT – *See* Taylorism.

SECRECY AGREEMENT – When the proprietor of some technological know-how lets somebody else have access to it, for research or evaluation purposes, it's called a "secrecy agreement". When the know-how is handed over for use in actual commerce, though, the agreement is a "know-how licence" – and many more of these are now in existence, thanks to the increasing impossibility of one corporation, however wealthy, developing all the know-how it needs in-house.

SEGMENTATION – A word on every management's lips – at least it should be. Segments make all the difference in today's markets. Even the giant that covers the whole gamut can't do so effectively without the right strategies for separate segments – in any one of which the giant, these days, can meet highly effective competition from smaller firms. That demands careful analysis of the business to determine how it actually does break down.

The analyst can list the different products on one side of a square and the different customers on the adjacent axis of the rectangle. For instance, a paint company may be selling its heavy duty product to shipbuilders and chemical plants. The blank spaces left in the square might raise the possibility of selling to, say, the do-it-yourself market.

The segmentor can also compare the size of each segment with the company's own position – showing where efforts should be redoubled and where, maybe, he should get out. The purpose of segmentation is always the same – to get the most out of the market and the company's strengths. But you can cut up the cake in many ways.

Looking at the market rather than the firm, for instance, you can segment by objectives – in Kenichi Ohmae's definition, "the different ways different customers use the product". This can yield important clues as to where to position your own offering. Segmentation by customers, combined with the identification of their needs, is an even more powerful tool. Ohmae cites the example of a facsimile equipment maker who had segmented his customers by product – high-speed machines or low speed. Segmentation by size showed very few large companies among the buyers for either type.

Why? The reason was that the slow and fast machines couldn't be linked in the national networks that these large customers required. So the maker was led to add a medium-speed machine to its line, successfully giving it a range of products for local, regional, and national customers.

There's one catch about segments, though. A company can easily persuade itself that it's the Czar of the Segment when actually it's drawn the lines round the area so tightly as to exclude everybody else – and its overall position is acutely and dangerously weak. The segmentation exercise isn't a cosmetic one: it should be a catapult to launch the company forward to greater success. (*See also*: Position.)

SENSITIVITY ANALYSIS – Nothing to do with sensitivity training. If you're making an estimate of, say, the outcome of a new enterprise on which you've set your heart, it's wise to find out how sensitive your plan is to what error. In other words, how great a fall in sales, margins, or both could the project afford before it ceases to be viable, attractive, or worth even a moment's thought? Often, a malfunction in just one variable is enough to sink the whole ship.

SET-UP TIME – The time taken to get a machine ready (hence, "make-ready") for production when the items being produced, or their specifications, are changed. This is one of manufacturers' huge hidden costs. One of the giant advantages of flexible manufacturing systems and other modern methods is that they greatly facilitate changeovers and reduce set-up (or make-ready) time to the minimum. A great deal of wasted set-up time, though, isn't the result of obsolete manufacturing methods, but of obsolete, sloppy management. (*See also*: FMS/FMC; Downtime.)

SHAREHOLDERS' EQUITY – The same as the "invested capital" of the company, i.e., the total capital less the debts owed to banks and fixed interest lenders. The return on this shareholders' equity is used as a prime measure of performance in US corporations, but can be most misleading.

Because of the impact of gearing, the firm with high debt will produce higher profits on the shareholders' equity than the identical firm with no debt – for just as long as the return on total capital stays above the net cost of the interest. But the basic performance of the indebted and the no-debt firm is no different – and many a company with a high return on equity has been concealing very poor performance on figures that count far more. (*See also*: Gearing.)

SHARE OPTION – Share option schemes vary considerably, with the main common features arising from the need to comply with tax law. But all revolve around the same principle of giving an executive the option to buy at a future date, if he so wishes, a fixed amount of shares at a price fixed in relation to the current market price when the option was granted. When the option matures, the holder, if the shares have risen, exercises the option and pockets his profit – and everybody's happy, especially the holder. If the shares have stayed put, or fallen, the option doesn't get exercised. So it's heads the executive wins, tails he doesn't lose – even if the shareholders do.

In theory, this acts as an incentive for management people (especially top management) to maximise their efforts so that the shareholders benefit through an enhanced share price. In practice, it has become a method for making top managers in top companies into rich men at the lowest possible risk and least possible cost to themselves – and with a debatable effect on incentives. In fact, one paradox is that it actually would pay the top management to run the corporation down to the point where its shares are heavily discounted. They could then grant themselves options, which would, of course, be worth vastly more after the company got back on trend.

Probably nobody's ever done that deliberately – but that's roughly what happened, all the same, at the big US car companies as slump turned to recovery in 1983. Cynics argue that the better managed the company, the tighter and meaner its option scheme will be. But where the option scheme is loose and over-generous, the chances of the system being changed from within are pretty remote. Why? Guess who proposes the share options . . .

SIMULATION – The representation, usually on a computer, of what will or may happen in real life if certain decisions are taken or certain eventualities result – say, from competitive action. The whole corporation can be approached in this way, or one very specific activity can be tested out. It's the scientific way of running an idea up a flagpole to see if anybody salutes. (*See also*: Modelling.)

SIS – Short-interval scheduling. If you're studying how to improve routine work (i.e., reduce its cost) by better planning and control, you can divide the work into small amounts that one worker can deal with in one short unit of time (an hour is usual); each amount of work is given to one worker, and each worker has performance checked regularly. The only trouble is that, while their performance will probably improve, the workers may get very bored – SIS flies in the face of more modern ideas. (*See also*: Job Enrichment.)

SKUNK WORKS – Outlying premises occupied by research and new-product development people, who are set free by the employing organisation to do their creative work. Once they've hit the jackpot, the skunk workers come in out of the cold. It's an attempt to escape from the bureaucratic straitjacket of the big corporation and to combine the benefits of flexibility and speed with those of the mammoth's marketing muscle and money.

SMART – A smart machine, as opposed to a dumb one, is a gadget that can do more than obey a single command or gesture. A light switch is dumb. A lighting console that adjusts light intensity to a predetermined level as external conditions change is smart – and likely to show much faster sales growth in today's markets.

Mostly, the smartness is microelectronic, and it's a fair bet that all dumb machines and instruments (which are as countless as the grains of sand on the beach) will be replaced in the fullness of time by smart ones. There's already a conspicuous example in the digital watch, which is smart enough to do many things beyond the power of a comparable clockwork mechanism.

The smart–dumb difference has moved to centre stage in management, and not just in manufacturing industry, because the smart machine holds the key to improvements in productivity and quality that would be impossible without microelectronic devices. The management that isn't exploring the full potential of the new smartness has only one word to describe it: dumb.

SOCIAL FORECASTING – Economic developments, especially in the field of marketing, commonly follow in the wake of social change – and not the other way around. Thus the boom that made Levi Strauss one of the most successful companies in the United States resulted not from the existence of factories making blue denim jeans, but from the changing social habits that made wearing the product both acceptable and popular. It follows that awareness of social trends is a powerful tool for planning corporate development of products and product portfolios. Wise companies therefore do social forecasting as a preliminary to their economic forecasts – and don't get stranded making the wrong product at the wrong time. (*See also*: Marketing Myopia.)

SPACE ARBITRAGE – The form of arbitrage which exploits the fact that, for example, a share is trading for less in New York than it is in London – so a sharp operator can make his killing by buying on Wall Street and simultaneously selling in Britain. The differences may be tiny, but the payoff can be huge. The "space" referred to is the geographic gap between the zones in which the fearless arbitrageur is hunting his profit. (*See also*: Arbitrage.)

SPAN OF CONTROL – How many people come under one other person's control. This used to loom very large in management theory and even in practice. The theorists held that beyond a certain number (usually seven), the span of control was too wide for effective management to be possible. The key word was "report": you were supposed not to have more than the magic number "reporting" to one manager.

There's obvious truth in the proposition that there must be a limit (imposed by available time, quite apart from anything else) in the numbers that one person can control. But that presupposes a hierarchic pyramid. In the more fluid organisations favoured today, with their heavy delegation of authority (as opposed to its heavy use), the one-to-seven ratio may not make any sense: anyway, the seven will be changing all the time with the change in the tasks that their boss has on his plate.

SPIN-OFF – When one line of business (say, building fighters for the Royal Air Force) gives birth to another business (say, using some of the aircraft technology for a new product for cars), that's a spin-off. The possibility of these uncovenanted marvels is often used to justify hefty spending on plainly uneconomic projects (like going to the moon or building Concorde). And in some cases, spin-off may even have resulted. Thus it's widely believed that the US world lead in microelectronics was a spin-off from the development work needed for military purposes. But most technological leads and leaps come about directly, not indirectly. Writers Derek French and Heather Saward have it right when they describe spin-off as "unplanned" and "usually minor". Unplanned things usually are.

SQC – Statistical quality control was the first Japanese breakthrough in management to be recognised in the West – though actually it's a Western technique, brought to Japan after the war and adopted by the locals with immense enthusiasm when they found what it could do: give much better control of quality at much lower cost.

SQC is based on sampling, the well-known branch of statistics without which political opinion polls and market research would never have got off the ground. Just as an opinion poll establishes the voting intentions of the entire electorate by questioning just a few of the voters, so checking a sample of parts, rather than all of them, enables the inspection department to get an accurate picture of what's happening to the entire run.

The technique is specialised but not especially sophisticated. It uses charts with upper and lower limits for statistical control. If the errors detected by sampling fall outside the limits predicted by statistical theory, you can immediately check to discover what's going wrong – and correct it. A second's thought will show that the savings must be huge compared to waiting until the defective part is built into a final product, which is then rejected (you hope) by a human inspector at the end of the line.

Nobody knows why SQC didn't catch on strongly in the West until the Japanese showed its value; long before that, the American high priest of SQC, Dr Frederick W. Deming, was a hero to the Japanese. Deming makes the point that effective use of SQC pays off in other ways, too – for example, in higher productivity as methods are tightened up and rejects fall. In fact, the Japanese have taken the possibilities of the technique far beyond statistics – into the heart of the management of the productive process.

The principle of stopping faults as soon as they occur has been carried back down the line, to stopping error before it can happen – by designing quality into the product and by making individual workers responsible for the total quality of everything on which they work. But there's nothing peculiarly Japanese about the excellence of the results. American managements that have now jumped on the Deming bandwagon are getting equal benefits – just as statistical theory would have predicted.

SREDIM – The method study part of TMS demands that you follow this sequence: *S*, for Select the job you're going to study; *R*, for Record the details of the job and the methods used to do it; *E*, for Examine the details with an eagle, critical eye; *D*, for Develop a better way; *I*, for Install the new and marvellous method; and *M*, for Maintain it – that is, keep it under study and modify as necessary in the interests of the object of the exercise, which is to achieve maximum efficiency. The sequence produces the mnemonic SREDIM. If that sounds too difficult to pronounce, spell it backwards – MIDERS. But don't *do* it backwards. (*See also*: TMS.)

STAFF – In strict theory, a staff executive or specialist has no operational responsibility, gives no orders to anybody (except his assistants and secretaries), and exists only to help the line managers as they go about the real business of the company. One definition of "staff relationship" even runs as follows: "Relationship between two members of an organisation one of whom looks to the other for advice and information, but neither of whom issues instructions to, or delegates authority to, the other."

In real life, it's not like that. When the staff people descended on operating units in the heyday of the conglomerates, the instructions flew around like rockets in Vietnam. Conversely, the staff is often at the receiving end of verbal battering and orderings-about from any line manager in a position to behave in that manner.

The truth is that, these days, line management can't exercise its responsibility and authority without heavy reliance on the so-called staff functions, while the latter are not much use unless they're deeply involved in the business and in its sharp-end results. As noted under general management, one of the strengths of the good Japanese company is that accountants, personnel managers, researchers, etc. are all expected to know the business of the business as thoroughly as the manager running it – that's why staff people can exchange jobs with line people with no difficulty in Japan: because there's no real difference. (*See also*: Line; General Management.)

STANDARD – The building bricks of control are standards, in particular for costs, but also for every other aspect of performance – such as quality, production rates, etc. The last two, however, obviously relate to cost, because the worse the performance on quality or output, the higher the costs will be. The difference between actuals and what should have been achieved is the deviation or variance from "standard costs".

A precise technical term, standard cost refers to the calculation in advance of what costs should be in predetermined circumstances. The figure is made up of several separate, accurate assessments: How much material is going to be used, and at what price; how much labour, and at what rates; and so forth. Obviously, you can't hope to run any manufacturing operation effectively without that knowledge – which you also need for valuing stocks and work in progress. But the technique for standard costing goes further than that.

Relate standard costs to standard prices, and you've got a control figure for the ultimate objective of the whole operation: to make money. But there's a world of difference between using standards for control and using them to set prices – the cost-plus system. That's starting from the wrong end, the right end being what the customer will pay, the traffic will bear, the market will stand – call it what you will.

The cost accountants thrive on other standards, too: the standard hour is the work produced in 60 minutes by an operator in ideal conditions; standard rating is what results from adding (a) a relaxation allowance to (b) the basic time needed for a job; standard time is (a) plus (b) plus (c), an allowance for additional work, plus (d) unoccupied time, or plain hanging about.

You can use these calculations for a standard time payment system – meaning that you pay the operator a wage rate per unit of time, multiplied by the standard time per unit, multiplied by the number of units he actually produces. He normally gets a minimum wage (standard time multiplied by wage rate) and is supposed to be galvanised into Herculean or Stakhanovite efforts by the extra factor.

The trouble is that the effort tends to run out when he's reached a predetermined level of earnings (predetermined by himself, that is). Anyway, the system is old-fashioned, unfashionable, and inappropriate in modern conditions. Standards, though, are none of these things. A modern business has measured standards for everything – and keeps them continuously high. (*See also*: Control; Cost Plus; Inventory; WIP.)

STOCHASTIC – Like it or not, know it or not, all business are stochastic systems. That is, what happens inside the firm is affected at random by things happening outside – above all, out there in the market. That's why managers have to resort to probabilities – because there are no certainties.

STRESS INTERVIEW – Some selectors think you can find out what you really need to know from a job applicant by bullying, goading, provoking, and attacking him or her in the interview. They're wrong.

SUB-OPTIMISATION – Falling short of the best possible combination of results: the natural condition of all companies all of the time. The difference between good and bad managers is that the former knows that his results are below the optimum and tries continuously and successfully to narrow the gap. The bad manager either thinks that his sub-optimisation is the optimum, or he is indifferent to the truth. Either way, his performance keeps on getting worse.

SUBORDINATE – Strictly speaking – and strictly's the word – a subordinate is somebody under the power and authority of a superior. These days, though, the order-and-obey relationship between superior and subordinate, or boss and bossed, is thought (rightly) to be less productive than the advise-and-consent relationship between senior and junior colleagues. It may (and should) come to the same thing – effective performance by people and also by their part of the organisation. But "advise and consent" means that you reach the destination by a more constructive – and distinctly more pleasant – route.

SUCCESSION PLAN – The most important question in management, after who's doing the job now, is who's going to do it next. In many cases, developing his own successor is one of the current man's prime duties. In others, higher management reserves the whole process of succession to itself.

Whichever approach is taken, the crucial point is that the succession is planned. There may even be a planning document, saying when each sitting tenant is expected to move on, together with who is expected to take his place (together with details of the heir-apparent's qualifications and experience).

If there's no successor in-house, the succession plan will note the fact, meaning (obviously) that a replacement will have to be recruited from outside. Only the most meticulously organised companies, with the largest budgets for personnel management, have planning of this kind, which smacks of bureaucracy. Still, it's better than the opposite extreme, which is to have no thought for succession at all. (*See also*: Management.)

SWITCH SELLING – Snaring a customer's interest by advertising a low price, and then by hook or by crook getting him or her to buy a more expensive version – maybe by saying (falsely) that the cheap one is sold out. Not done in the best of companies – only in the worst.

SWOT – Strengths, Weaknesses, Opportunities, Threats. If you know exactly what each of these are for your business, you have the key to the present and the future. Which is exactly why a SWOT analysis has become a basic element in the planning and marketing apparatus of many companies.

The value doesn't lie only in the facts that the analysis should lay bare, but in the attitude of mind which accepts that the company *does* have weaknesses as well as strengths, *does* face threats as well as opportunities. That acceptance isn't as negative as it sounds, because the awareness of weaknesses and threats provides an indispensable platform for giving the company positive strategies.

The latter won't work if they require resources in areas where the company is weak – unless the plan simultaneously takes in the repair of these disadvantages and their conversion to strengths. Plans won't make any sense, either, unless they take into account existing and potential threats to the company's position. The Detroit carmakers, for instance, weren't too clever in ignoring the threat posed by foreign producers making cars that consumed less petrol and cost fewer dollars.

The positive strategy, though, aims to use the strengths, existing or obtainable, to capitalise on the opportunities – as General Motors used its engineering and money muscle and worldwide spread to build a global product strategy in its counterattack. It goes without saying (or should) that the company must be as honest about its own virtues, and as clearheaded about its opportunities, as it is merciless about its weaknesses and threats.

Sometimes, just listing the SWOT elements will open up new vistas – by suddenly highlighting areas that had been overlooked. But beware of one thing. Knowing your own SWOT isn't enough: the best competitors do a SWOT analysis of their *rivals* too – because that's the best approach if you want to swat them flat.

SYNECTICS – A more directed form of brainstorming. It also rests on generating ideas by bringing together a group of people, and likewise operates on the no-holds-barred principle: all ideas, apparently relevant or not, are thrown into the pool while the people taking part look for connections among them, purposely using analogy and metaphor in the search for ideas that are really new.

The difference from brainstorming is that the synectics group is purposive: that is, it won't just spew forth ideas but will select from among them the best or likeliest few (or maybe even just one) for further development. Consultants specialising in this field use a similar method in helping companies come up with new product development. The groups are carefully chosen to provide several different angles of approach to the problem – or, rather, the opportunity. (*See also*: Brainstorming; Lateral Thinking.)

SYNERGY – Adding two and two together in business management to make five is no easier than it sounds. But that is what synergy (defined by the dictionary as "combined or correlated action of a group of bodily organs") was supposed to achieve in the heyday of the conglomerates – the Swinging Sixties, when management skills, sharpened in the business schools, were regarded as prime corporate assets, separate from the business or businesses to which the skills were applied.

That created, in theory, one form of synergy: the higher performance which resulted from applying superior central management powers to disparate businesses that couldn't have achieved the same progress and profits with their own inferior management abilities, or with their lesser power when it came to raising money or buying other businesses. In this sense, two and two were made into five because the whole (the brilliantly led conglomerate) was worth more than its parts.

In the eighties, which is tough on the theory, old conglomerates, good and bad alike, have been valued in the stock market at *less* than their individual businesses are worth. This synergy-in-reverse partly reflects the disillusion created by experience – the destruction by disappointing events of the notion of higher, infinitely transferable management skills. But that disillusion hasn't robbed synergy of its currency, although in another sense – that of complementing one operation or business with another, a process which, because of shared resources or technology or markets, can increase the effectiveness of both.

The concept differs from vertical and horizontal integration in being based on this pooling of key resources. Obviously, its value (and difficulty) lies not only in finding the synergistic opportunity, but in actually making the most (or anything) of it. Thus, pharmaceutical companies buying cosmetic houses have mostly made a mess of improving the cosmetic returns – even though there were obvious points of contact (in R&D and distribution). Either the synergy was less than the buyers believed, or the task of managing it was beyond them. But that management task is in fact clearly set out by that dictionary definition – "combined or correlated action". The word ultimately means no more than effective coordination of the business centre and all its parts. In achieving that, its two and two may not add up to five, but the company will add up to something capable of coping with an age where single-capacity management is no longer enough. (*See also*: Horizontal Integration; Vertical Integration.)

SYSTEMS 1, 2, 3, AND 4 – Another great name in social science, Rensis Likert, came up with no less than four descriptions of managerial style in his work at the Institute of Social Research at the University of Michigan. The descriptions were "exploitative-authoritative", "benevolent-authoritative", "consultative", and "participating group", which later became Systems 1, 2, 3 and 4, because of the risk that the far less neutral epithets would affect the attitudes of managers during research.

The overlaps between the social science of behavioural approaches to management are inevitably many and large. System 1 is the same as authoritarian management, Douglas McGregor's Theory X; System 4 doesn't mean anything different from McGregor's Theory Y. Both, too, have correspondences with the 9:1 ("authority-obedience") and 9:9 ("team management") positions in Blake and Mouton's managerial grid. Likert has gone two better than McGregor, though, by coming up with terms for intermediate stages between Theory Y and Theory X – though even that doesn't truly exhaust the real-life permutations and combinations. (*See also*: Managerial Style; Theory X and Theory Y; Managerial Grid.)

T

TASK FORCE – A term stolen from naval nomenclature to cover any small group of managers who are brought together for a specific task – usually one of some urgency or importance. The members are generally detached from other duties for as long as the task takes – though if it takes too long, the task force evolves into some other form of corporate life.

The device has become more common as the variety, complexity, and unpredictability of corporate problems have increased, along with the need to get a speedy resolution of whatever has to be done – from a crash new-product launch to a change in management accounting practices. Task forces also have a specific meaning in systems of management by objectives. They're formed to examine how performance can be improved – as it always can be. (*See also*: MBO.)

TAYLORISM – The "scientific management" ideas of Frederick Winslow Taylor (1856–1915), an engineer who worked in the American steel industry, were widely hailed on their appearance; in 1910, one witness before a tribunal argued that if the US railroads followed Taylor's methods, they would save £1 million a day. He was probably right, too – and the witness would probably have been just as right half a century later.

Scientific management to Taylor meant, first, using analysis and experiment, just like a scientist, to work towards the best method of operation in any industrial activity; second, choosing and educating workers to use the optimum methods developed; third, achieving management and worker cooperation so that the best methods were used to obtain the best results for all parties.

Subsequently, the first two aspects of Taylorism were stressed and the third ignored. Peter Drucker has drawn attention to the injustice of pillorying Taylor as a heartless efficiency expert who sought to reduce men to the level of machines. Actually, the great theorist wrote that "The principal object of management should be to secure the maximum prosperity for the employer, *coupled with the maximum prosperity for the employee.*"

That was the end towards which Taylor and the followers who developed his ideas into modern work study were striving. Perhaps the critics who attacked the Taylorists for inhumanity weren't so much concerned about effectiveness as by the war against the boss class. Taylor was right: it's a phoney war. (*See also*: Work Study.)

TECHNOLOGY TRANSFER – Not transfer between companies (which is licensing), but the far more difficult task of transferring technological know-how between parts of the same company. It sounds easy, and should be; but the organisational barriers can be almost insurmountable.

One newish idea is to appoint a very senior executive as technology czar, with the job not only of ensuring that the corporation has all the technology it requires (and is working on what it will require), but that the parts of the corporation where the technology is lodged make it known and available to other divisions – as, these days, it must be to optimise results. (*See also*: Licensing.)

TEROTECHNOLOGY – Never mind the word, consider the question: when should you replace a piece of plant? When is it no longer worth maintaining the old, and worthwhile switching to something newer and more productive? Terotechnology is the discipline that gives you the answer – the word comes from the Greek *terein* and means, simply, the technology of care.

The manager needs to know how much plant and machinery

will cost over its economic life and how much it will consume in resources. He must also have clear information on the maintenance and performance of his machines – and the buildings that contain and support them. The data are tools for the effective management of what is a crucial side of any manufacturing business.

While the terotechnological equations are complex, one management principle for the eighties isn't. Even if replacing an old machine looks uneconomic, not replacing it could be deadly if the new technology gives an advantage in the marketplace or in manufacturing costs. An old piece of equipment should be regarded as guilty (i.e., obsolete or obsolescent) until it's proved innocent – and providing the proof is partly terotechnology's job.

TF – Technological forecasting. Producing future developments in technology has become, very obviously, more and more important every year. It hasn't become any easier – even the best efforts are seldom more than half right. That recalls the famous observation of soap tycoon Lord Leverhulme that half the money he spent on advertising was wasted.

As in that case, so with TF: you never know which half. TF was the real theme of Ted Levitt's famous essay, "Marketing Myopia": typically (and it's no criticism of Levitt), his own essays into TF (on the imminent development of practical fuel cells, for example) proved wrong. In the effort to do better, forecasters have developed many techniques – like the Delphi method and brainstorming.

The problem, though, lies not in the methodology but in the imperfect knowledge of which – and, more important, when – emergent technologies will pay off. If anybody knew which developments would lead nowhere, those developments would cease at once. Since nobody does know, sensible TF is like a great football team's game plan: it covers all the options. (*See also*: Marketing Myopia; Delphi Method; Brainstorming.)

THEORY X AND THEORY Y – Certainly the most widely known of behavioural management theses. The work of Douglas McGregor contrasted two types of companies. The first (X) was built round the idea that nobody works unless they have to or are made to. The alternative theory (Y) holds that, on the contrary, people love to work and, given the right conditions, will strive to do their very best.

The Theory-X company thus relies on order-and-obey, stick-and-carrot, hire-and-fire to achieve its objectives by making people conform to them. Supervision is constant, and workers are left with little room in which to use their initiative. Theory-X companies are thus not nice, and very tough.

Theory-Y companies, on the other hand, are very nice: and if there is an iron hand, it's thickly concealed by the velvet glove. In this theory, people are disposed to work as much as they are to watch football. Giving them as much room as possible for initiative and responsibility enhances their performance, and does away with the need for strict supervision – indeed, you may be able to do without supervision altogether.

The battle of behaviour has been going all Theory Y's way – it's deeply unfashionable to manage in X-style, deeply fashionable (quality of working life, quality circles, participation, etc.) to adopt the Y approach – sanctified in Robert Townsend's best-selling book *Up The Organisation*. But even though X is out, that doesn't solve the problem of how you can have X-type toughness with a Y-type company.

That isn't a problem in Japan, where disciplined X-traditions combine with enormous Y-type emphasis on maximising the satisfaction of the workers. With more and more US firms trying to copy the Japanese in these respects, a lot of managers are going to learn that motivation isn't achieved by permissiveness alone.

The truth behind the X–Y spectrum isn't the obvious (but useful) insight that people's own internal drives and desires are better motivators than external whips and spurs. In fact, many elements of Theory-X companies are present in Theory Y: for example, fear of demotion or even dismissal for inadequate performance (an emotional drive which is both internal and external).

No – the real point is to draw attention to the vital matter of the culture of the organisation. Does it support and encourage personal and thus corporate achievement? If it does, whether you call it X, Y, or Z hardly matters. If it doesn't, resign.

T-GROUP – This kind of get-together, or study group, was at its peak of popularity when interpersonal relationships were a major preoccupation of management. The T (for training) Group consists of a small number of people who meet under a trainer to discuss and analyse their behaviour towards each other, and their reactions to that behaviour, during the sessions.

This "sensitivity training" has obvious affinities with group analysis, EST (Erhard Seminar Therapy), and other soul-baring assemblies. Like EST and its variants, it has been criticised for producing trauma in the over-sensitive. Like them, too, it's suspect on the grounds that, however great the short-term effects may seem, in the longer term, those effects tend to be dead.

THERBLIG – Not a Norwegian troll, but the name used for work elements (like search, find, select, grasp, hold, transport, load position, assemble). You need this kind of analysis for work study, which is helped by giving each therblig (there are seventeen in all) its own symbol and colour. The idea is to enhance performance, cut down on wasteful motion and use of time, and generally facilitate efficiency.

Why therblig? That's Gilbreth spelled backwards – Frank B. of that name being the scientific management expert who carried on the torch handed over by Frederick W. Taylor. Gilbreth worked with his much younger wife Lillian. You can tell how many children they had by the title of a book about them, *Cheaper by the Dozen*. (*See also*: Work Study.)

THREE-D THEORY – One up on the managerial grid, adding to the latter's two dimensions (concern for production and concern for people). The three-D designer, William J. Reddin, calls the latter "tasks orientation" and "relationships orientation", which looks like no improvement. What he adds, though, is "effectiveness", defined as how well the manager hits the performance targets he is asked to achieve. Reddin is obviously right in his adding up. Concern for production or people without performance may be pretty, but it is also pretty useless. (*See also*: Managerial Grid.)

TIME-SPAN OF DISCRETION – How long can you spend on your job before somebody in higher authority checks up on your performance? If it's about one minute, your time-span of discretion is very low. If it's once a year, when, say, an all-powerful general manager meets his chief executive, his time-span of discretion is very high – and he will expect to be remunerated accordingly.

This method of job classification was devised by Elliott Jacques, an industrial psychologist, as one of the many more-or-less doomed attempts to institute order in the untidy systems for establishing pay differentials. Note that the time-span isn't that of the individual, but goes with the job. Whatever the time-span, Person A may in practice be given longer discretion than Clot B. (*See also*: Job Description; Job Evaluation.)

TMS – Time-and-motion study is the discipline basic to the scientific management school, or Taylorism. It really is a discipline, too: the systematic examination, analysis, and measurement of how work is performed in order to get better methods that occupy less time. It's the time study bit of TMS where the famous or infamous stop watch comes in: the job is broken down into "elements", each of which is timed precisely. This presupposes that the methods being used are the best possible. It's no use having an operative do two elements in a two-minute standard operating time if they could be combined, by better methods, into a single element taking one minute. For that, you need SREDIM. (*See also*: SREDIM; Taylorism.)

TNC – Transnational corporation. What all MNC's (multinational corporations) would become if the managements believed their own publicity. Like the MNC, the TNC operates in many countries. Unlike the MNC, though, it doesn't draw its

management mainly from one country in which ultimate management control is also vested.

So far, there have been precious few examples of this genus,
since what national managements and shareholders have, they
prefer to hold. The main exceptions are companies created by
transnational mergers – like Unilever or Royal Dutch Shell. Even
so, what usually happens is that the two nationalities jointly
dominate just as much as the single nationality in a US-owned
MNC. But this chapter in world economic history is still being
written – and the trend, for many reasons (good ones, too) is
plainly towards real transnationalism. (*See also*: MNC.)

TRADE CREDIT – The time a supplier allows before he expects to
be paid – usually thirty days after shipment. Sharp firms milk
trade credit to the utmost and beyond. Stupid firms use it to
finance their business. Both are in the wrong – the first because
it's bad behaviour, the second because they often go broke.

TRADE CYCLE – The trade or business cycle governs corporate
results to a far greater extent than corporate management is prone
to admit. The world and national economies have their cycles
from peak to trough, and so do individual industries, some (like
steel) far more than others – and the different cycles, while they
influence one another, never completely coincide.

What causes the cycles is a controversy that has kept econom-
ists happily disputing for decades – there's even a school of
thought (if that's the right phrase) attributing these eight- to
ten-year cycles to sunspots. More likely is the impact of surges in
investment, sometimes following political upheavals – like the
huge catch-up required in production of civilian goods after
World War II.

The impact of investment can be seen most clearly in mined
and extracted commodities. Shortage fears and high prices (like
those of oil after 1973) encourage investment, which adds to
supply at a time when the high prices (like those of oil) are curbing
demand. When the new capacity comes in, the result is mammoth

surpluses (like those of oil) and pressure on prices (like those of oil).

The vital need for the manager is to remember, as experts (like those of oil companies) often forget, that what goes up must come down – and vice versa. Scenario planning should always bear in mind that today's boom will at some point become tomorrow's bust. Bets on everlasting booms have seldom paid – just ask anyone who lost his shirt on computer shares in the seventies. (*See also*: Scenario Planning.)

TRADE-OFF – The basic concept of business planning is that you can't normally have your cake and eat it. No corporation can hope, for example, to have the highest volume and highest prices, on one hand, and the lowest promotion, customer service and development costs on the other. To maintain its abnormal market dominance, it will have to spend on the latter activities – and that's the trade-off.

The most common form of trade-off used to be that involving volume, price and quality. If you went for the first, you expected to sell at low prices and to offer low quality. But new production methods and new demands in markets have changed the balance radically. Indeed, the company that throws quality into the trade-off pot may find itself being traded-off as the customers move elsewhere.

TRADING PROFIT – *See* Operating Profit.

TRADING UP AND DOWN – Getting a higher price for a higher perceived value of a product is the name of the game in modern markets. Western manufacturers were left with little option but to trade up, given that rivals in the Far East could always undercut them if they tried the opposite tactic of trading down – that is, lowering the price and probably the quality of the product or service to attract a lower segment of the market.

The catch, of course, is that if everybody is trying to trade up, it may become a game in which nobody is winning. Trading up and down aren't the only alternatives, anyway. Companies can get the benefit of trading down – greatly widening their markets and sales potential, without sacrificing quality or profitability, as the learning curve works and as economies of scale come into play – as in the calculator, computer, and integrated circuit markets.

An entire company can trade up – that is, seek to move its image and that of its products up-market. The conspicuous example is the effort by Ford Motor to escape from an association with cheap, basic motoring (which dates back to the Model-T) and establish itself in the higher-priced, higher-profit sectors of the market. As the Ford example shows, it's not an easy task, it can take decades and it's liable to setback as with the Edsel, the most unsuccessful car launch in history. (*See also*: Learning Curve; Economies of Scale; Game Theory.)

TRANSFER PRICING – The price at which goods are transferred from one part of a company to another presents one of the trickiest problems in management. It has no perfect solution. If you charge only costs, that removes any profit incentive from the supplying division – and makes it impossible to judge whether it should be making the thing at all.

If you go to the other extreme, and charge a true, arm's-length market price, you forfeit the advantage of having an in-house supply – and (because the purchasing division will apply its own mark-up on a higher base) you may push the final price to the consumer up to uncompetitive levels. That actually happened to multidivisional companies in which several transfers took place before the product reached the market. (A 15% markup, applied each time a product changes hands, doubles the price after five transfers.)

Most companies opt for a solution somewhere between the two extremes – and sometimes have to settle bitter disputes about the transfer price between warring divisions. The only certain points are that (a) the overall benefit to the corporation should be paramount, and (b) if the system demands complex and constant intervention by several people, there's something wrong with the system – and it should be changed.

TRANSPORTATION PROBLEM – Nothing to do with being unable to get a taxi on a rainy night. It's a technical term referring to what the business mathematicians call an "allocation problem" – in this case, how to shift divided holdings of parts or raw materials or finished goods, at least cost, to the points where they are wanted.

TRIAL BALANCE – The acid test of double-entry bookkeeping, in which every transaction, in the system invented by the medieval Italians, is entered in the ledger twice – once as a credit, once as a debit. Since the two sides of the ledger should always be the same, the accountant doing the trial balance adds them up – and hopes that balance they will. If they don't, the feathers fly.

TURNAROUND – Turning around a company that's apparently suffering from a terminal disease sounds like one of the toughest tasks in management. It can also be one of the easiest ways of making an executive's personal fortune. So long as the company has a business worth anything, the turnaround man – if he's good at the job – has it made.

While the business still has value, but is losing money, the company will be priced in the stock market far below that underlying worth of the operation. Take a company losing £2 million on £20 million of sales; chop out £3 million of costs by mass firings, selling assets to reduce the debt-equity ratio, and improving basic efficiency, and you've got profits of £1 million on these sales of £20 million. Though 5% on sales is still pretty feeble, the profit the turnaround man will show on his share options will be marvellous.

Turnarounds are the speciality of company doctors. The biggest and best on record have been in the car industry – the job Ernest R. Breech did on Ford after the war, and the equally heroic recent performance of Lee Iacocca at Chrysler. Rubbing in the point, Iacocca's compensation arrangements brought him $2.6 million in 1982–83 – and from the shareholders' angle, that was a bargain. (*See also*: Debt-Equity Ratio; Company Doctor.)

TURNKEY CONTRACT – If you want a new plant, you can run the show yourself, employing contractors for the various types of work required; or you can order everything from one specialist (a Bechtel, Fluor or Lummus, say) and let him get on with it. Then all you have to do, when the project is complete and handed over, is turn the key, hope all systems are "go", and pay the bill.

TURNOVER – A double meaning here, one far more important than the other. The most common and least important usage is sales revenue. Apart from being the number that determines your ranking in the *Times* 1000, it tells you very little about a company unless you already know a great deal more – like the profit margin earned on those sales and the amount of capital needed to finance them. That brings in the second meaning of turnover: how fast capital, or stock, or anything else, is "turned over" in the course of a year. Thus, if a business does £1 million in sales but carries a £1 million inventory, it turns over its stock once a year, and is lucky to be alive.

The Japanese have produced fantastic figures for stock turnover and, as a result, for turnover of total capital employed. The relationship to ROCE is obvious. If a firm earns 5% on £1 million in sales and turns over a capital of £500,000 twice in a year, its ROCE figure will be 10% – a miserable number, too.

Double the rate of capital turnover, though, by doubling the sales or halving the capital, or some combination of both, and you double the ROCE. That's the driving rationale behind vigorous asset management in a policy which has been called LIMO – least input for the most output.

There is a third meaning of turnover, actually: applied to labour, it means the percentage of the work force that leaves during the year and has to be replaced. Like stock turnover, it needs careful watching. Too high a percentage almost certainly means that the company is doing something very wrong and paying handsomely for the privilege. (*See also*: ROCE/ROI; ROS; Asset Management; Labour Stability Index.)

TWO-TIER BOARD – The system, established by law in West Germany (the *Aufsichtsrat* and *Vorstand*), that separates the directors into two bodies: the executives and, above them, the supervisory board, which appoints the executives and invigilates their performance. As (in theory) happens with the one-tier or "unitary board", the top tier is elected by the shareholders (though the workers may join in). But the separation of the tiers means that the identification of the top tier with shareholders' interests is more real (or should be) than when the executives and non-executives sit cheek by jowl on the unitary board. (*See also*: Aufsichtsrat; Vorstand.)

U

UNAIDED RECALL – A method of market research (or, more accurately, advertising research) in which the interviewer asks the interviewee which ads he can recall. This so-called spontaneous recall is valued very highly by ad men – but it doesn't actually tell you anything about the one vital question: whether the ad has increased the interviewee's propensity to pay good money for the thing being advertised.

USP – The unique selling proposition is one of the few management terms to have emerged from the advertising industry, whose service to the cause of management is largely by the lip – and not much of that, either. But Rosser Reeves of the Ted Bates agency won immortality (and many millions) by insisting that all advertisements should give consumers a clear and unique reason why they should purchase the product.

While the force of the USP approach in advertising is evident (really, self-evident), the acronym has moved into general management use because of its equally strong relevance to product development and planning. The evidence is overwhelming that products which are "me too" – offering no real difference – not only aren't going to make it easy to write ads; they're also going to make themselves very hard to sell in general.

V

VALUE ADDED – This isn't just added value in reverse; it's the same concept seen from the only viewpoint that ultimately counts – the customer's. The more value is added – for example, by convenience, features, or performance – the higher the price the customer will be prepared to pay. Which means, inevitably, that the added value (the difference between the basic costs and the realised price) will be optimised.

This process has become mandatory in market after market in recent years, simply because, as potential supply has exceeded demand, so only those suppliers able to achieve high differentiation have been able to charge high (or higher) prices. That has become the only real way to add value to the whole business.

VALUE ANALYSIS – Crudely put, tearing a product to pieces to see how it can be put together more effectively – that is, more cheaply or in a way that will increase customer appeal, or (preferably) both. This is a team job: every function within the firm that has a contribution to make is called in.

That's essential because the VA work looks at materials, manufacturing methods, and basic design in the effort to achieve a better result. Any component, any material, any design feature may be costing more than the value that it is contributing to the final product. More often than not, the VA team will substitute simpler designs, parts, and procedures for unnecessarily complex ones – and the answer may not be one depending on new or high technology.

Another common result is to substitute cheaper materials without losing value – in the case of car components made out of plastic instead of steel, for example, the cheaper material may enhance the value by lightness and by easier, cheaper replacement in case of damage.

The process of applying VA is called VE – value engineering; it should really be built into the fabric of the firm. VA is one of the most valuable techniques around, which makes it more than somewhat mysterious that top management has rarely taken the philosophy to its bosom.

VALUE ENVELOPE – When plotting the network for some project or other, the planner charts what would happen if all stages were completed as quickly as possible. He also plots what would happen if they were all completed in the longest possible time – as slowly as allowable. The difference between the two is the value envelope. If the weekly charting of progress shows that the project is going outside the envelope, that's when you call on the troops, the fire brigade, and anybody else who might help to get the project back on the rails – or, rather, back inside the envelope. Even if you're not using networks, the logical principle of measuring the worst possible result against the best possible outcome is an excellent guide to both decision making and control of execution. (*See also*: Network.)

VALUE TO THE BUSINESS – Whichever is less, the amount you could get by selling an asset, or the net cost of replacing it, is the worth (or value) of that asset to the business – that is, it tells you how much you'd be out of pocket if a blast furnace, say, blows up or gets stolen (not an easy thing to happen with a blast furnace, but still).

VARIABLE – The opposite of fixed: variable costs are those which go up and down – with production, for example. If you make less, you will use less materials, and vice versa. That makes sense – but paradoxically, if the cost per unit *doesn't* vary as activity levels change, that's a *variable* cost. For instance, if a product contains 50p of plastic, it will always do so, whether you make 100,000 units or one. But the *overall* cost will be highly variable: £50,000 or 50p.

Now, if the cost per unit *does* vary with the level of operations, that's a *fixed* cost – thus, if you're paying £100,000 rent and making 100,000 units, the rent per unit is £1: double output and the figure comes down to 50p: but the *overall* cost will stay the same; it will be fixed, come what may, at £100,000.

VARIANCE – Anybody who expects budgets to come out as originally drafted is certainly no businessman, and probably a fool. The variance (usually given in a separate column in the management accounts) highlights problem areas for the management to consider – why have profits fallen (or, often more significantly, risen) more than expected? If the variance is negative, what's being done to correct the deficiency? Variance reporting is the basis of the technique known as management by exception, since it's the major variances that draw management's attention to areas of concern.

It's well worth remembering, though, that variance-free figures can conceal more worrying problems than those highlighted by variances. The smoothly flowing operation may have been smoothed with malice aforethought – by managers delaying or accelerating expenditure, for example. The operation whose results are wildly adrift from budget may just have been badly budgeted. But even so, you need to find the reason *why*. That's the question every variance should spark.

VARIANT – *See* Product Line.

VENTURE – "Venture management" and "venture capital" came into increasing use as existing businesses were tried and found wanting in their ability to generate new business within their bureaucratic walls. The word "venture" first became current in these fortresses – Du Pont used it to describe supposedly autonomous groups set up to develop independent projects. But the culture of the corporation and that of the true entrepreneur fitted as well as square pegs and round holes.

Venture fled from the big corporation – as did many of the entrepreneurs who proceeded to attract "venture" capital. That means money that accepts a high degree of downside risk (including total loss) in return for an exceptionally high degree of upside potential. Since most such ventures are in high technology, venture and its capitalists have become inseparably linked with places like Silicon Valley.

Actually, a venture is no different from any other kind of start-up investment – except that the venture capitalist takes a closer interest in the management of the venture concerned than is customary among financiers, and that the venture capital firms also draw their investors from wider sources. Big corporations have now entered the game, too, because it's become increasingly clear that, in the evolution of modern markets and modern products, an old saying has a new and threatening meaning: nothing ventured, nothing gained.

VERTICAL INTEGRATION – Just as big companies have a built-in urge to expand by lateral or horizontal integration (acquiring related businesses) so they tend to find vertical integration irresistible. The most common vertical direction is backwards; that sounds Irish, but it means going back down the supply chain until the limit is reached – when the company controls production of all the raw materials and all the semi-manufactures and parts made from them for final assembly into the finished product.

The acme of vertical integration is an oil company that owns the crude oil, the tankers that transport it, the refineries that process it, and the petrol stations that sell the end-products. In other businesses, vertical integration has become less popular – there's no percentage in owning your own steel or fastener plants if they're too small, inefficient or obsolescent to compete with outside suppliers.

Modern managements try to achieve the benefits of vertical integration (assurance of supply, quality control, flexibility, maximum added value) by establishing close relationships with arm's-length suppliers – so close in Japan that the supplier becomes "one of the family". Techniques like *kanban* and SQC have made it unnecessary to tie up resources back down the line in what by definition isn't the company's main line of business.

But there's also forward vertical integration – where a company moves down the line towards the point of sale, buying its customers or competing with them. The forward variety is stronger in modern conditions than the backward – companies often feel that they can't develop enough sensitivity to the market, or maximise their sales and profits, unless they control their own outlets, or some of them.

For two reasons, it's a difficult strategy to pull off. First, the company isn't a retailer or wholesaler, by definition, and has to master a wholly new business. Second, if it is competing with its customers, they won't like the competition. The difficulties explain why, more or less simultaneously, Xerox was closing down its office equipment shops while IBM was opening its own "product centres". All firms beyond a certain size will have some degree of vertical integration: the trick is not to have too much, in either direction. (*See also*: Acquisition; Kanban; SQC.)

VERTICAL PRODUCT/MARKET SELECTION – The opposite, or complement, to horizontal product/market selection. The vertical choice of a product or market involves moving up or down the market concerned. Thus, a maker of luxury cars like Mercedes-Benz chooses to move down into a more compact type of car and a lower price bracket. Generally, the exercise of options in this area results in increased vertical integration – that is, the company makes more of the materials/components it uses, or gets involved in more downstream manufacture using the components or products it currently produces. (*See also*: Horizontal Product/Market Selection; Vertical Integration.)

VORSTAND – The executive directors of a West German company – the people appointed by the supervisory *Aufsichtsrat* to run the company. They have a fixed term of five years, but that isn't inviolable. The supervisors can fire *Vorstand* members (whose salaries they fix) for serious personal misconduct or mismanagement of the company's affairs. That doesn't happen very often – but it's a stronger and better institutionalised form of sanction than the practice in most British boardrooms. (*See also*: Aufsichtsrat.)

W

WAGE DRIFT – What usually happens to pay after rates are fixed by bargaining (with or without negotiating difficulty) is that the workers actually earn more than they should, according to the rates agreed. The gap between negotiated and actual pay is the wage drift, made up of all sorts of special payments and allowances. The efficient firm monitors the gap very carefully and continuously to ensure that its system is working properly, that its labour costs are under control – and that it's not being had.

WASTING ASSET – If an asset isn't going to last for ever (or, say, fifty years, which is for ever to an accountant), it's going to waste away – because, once its useful life is over, its only value is as scrap. The financial consequences of wasting away are dealt with by the device of depreciation. You may find it difficult to think of an asset that doesn't waste. Generally speaking, there's only one: land. (*See also*: Depreciation.)

WHITE KNIGHT – When a company has mismanaged itself to the point where its mismanagers can't resist a hostile takeover bid, their best and only hope is to find a friendlier fellow to pay more – as Gulf Oil did with SOCAL, for example, in the biggest ($13.2 billion) merger in history. The name suggests the gallant vision of a Sir Galahad or a Saint George galloping along to save the tremulous virgin from the evil dragon. But many a rescued corporate maiden has awakened to find that her knight is actually a dragon in disguise.

WIP – Work-in-progress. The acid test of effective plant management is the length of time it takes to convert materials and components into finished goods. The shorter the time, obviously, the less the cost of carrying stock, the faster the realisation of cash for the product, and the greater the prospects of winning orders (because delivery times will be more competitive, as well as costs). In poorly run plants, it can take 100 times as long to get work-in-progress through the plant as it does actually to machine the product. Worse still, many managements don't know either that awful fact, or how long the process is actually taking in their own probably benighted operation. (*See also*: Inventory.)

WORK STUDY – "I'm a time study man, and a time study man must study time" – so ran a famous song from the musical, *The Pajama Game*. But it's fairly foolish to work out how long an operation should take unless you're sure that the operation is being done properly in the first place.

That involves method study. Once you've established the best way of making the widget, you can then measure how long each stage in widget manufacture should take by time study. But these days, such time-honoured techniques of scientific management are being overtaken by new production technology, which, because it uses machines rather than men, can be relied upon to deliver the goods without the aid of a stop-watch. (*See also*: TMS.)

WORKING CAPITAL – Means what it says – net current assets required for the company to carry on with its work. Technically, it's the surplus of a firm's current assets over its current liabilities. Lack of sufficient working capital is what lays companies low when they've been overtrading. Abundance of the stuff is beautiful at all times. (*See also*: Current; Overtrading.)

Y

YIELD – The returns in ROCE (return on capital employed) and ROI (return on investment) are both yields – although the latter word is more commonly used on the Stock Exchange, referring to the dividend as a percentage of the price of the stock. The principle is exactly the same: dividing the income from an investment by the cost of that investment.

In management, a positive yield means exactly what it says: the investment is in profit, and the ratio has a plus sign up front. A negative yield is a loss: i.e., some of the capital invested is being consumed. A yield rate is another way of talking about the internal rate of return (IRR).

It's a good word, yield – conveying the suggestion that management projects are supposed to bear fruit, not just to sit there looking pretty. (*See also*: IRR.)

Z

ZBB – The technique of zero-based budgeting is the only management concept ever to be linked with a politician, and a president of the United States, at that. Since the president was Jimmy Carter, who tried to apply the technique as governor of Georgia, but didn't get very far with it in Washington, political identification isn't much help to acceptance of a difficult idea: that every function in an organisation is guilty, or rather unnecessary, until proved otherwise.

The ZB budgeter must start from the assumption that no budget for the function being budgeted exists, or ever has existed. Thus there is zero cost. If the budgeter wants to spend money on a given function, he must justify the spending in terms of the benefit it will confer. As that suggests, this is rather tedious as a way of budgeting for activities that everybody knows quite well must be carried out – but it does have a far less tedious aspect.

That's the idea of evaluating every piece in the corporation machinery at regular intervals and asking, Do we really need to do this at all? If the answer is yes, the next question is pretty obvious: How much is it worth spending to get what we want? Organisations customarily don't ask these questions, because the answers can be very uncomfortable. Really, though, ZBB isn't much use without ZBA – zero-based administration, a concept that seeks to establish, right across the board, how much a company needs to spend, at the minimum, on administration, so as to meet the corporate, divisional and functional objectives.

Of course, that implies that these objectives have been formed. Nor is ZBA the only way to get the best VFM (value for money). Another approach is to make functional departments charge internal users for their services – and for the users to have the right to argue the bill if they aren't getting VFM. They should be.

ZERO DEFECTS – This approach to quality performance, born in the mid-sixties, was a false dawn. It sprang from the defence industry, based on the idea that statistical quality control, with its toleration of a small number of defects as an AQL (acceptable quality level) encouraged slackness.

Instead, the ZD programmes attempted to eliminate faults by making the objective no defects at all. The techniques were motivational, with encouragement backed by cash incentives – but their adoption wasn't general, and the initial movement was made obsolete by the Japanese combination of SQC with design for quality and making workers responsible for the total quality of the workpiece (not just the bit they worked on themselves).

Curiously enough, you'll still see ZD on the identification tags of Japanese workers. It's very much alive. For while the quality control techniques have virtually eliminated defects, the ZD philosophy is preserved for its motivational value; joining such newcomers as "right first time" in keeping up the pressure for better performance. (*See also*: SQC.)

ZERO-SUM GAME – *See* Game Theory.

ACKNOWLEDGEMENTS

Any book of definitions relies on the work of previous toilers in the field: I am especially grateful for the excellent contributions to clarity of managerial expression made by Derek French and Heather Saward (*Dictionary of Management*, Gower) and R. G. Anderson (*A Dictionary of Management Terms*, Macdonald & Evans). Other useful compilations include *The Encyclopaedia of Management*, edited by Carl Heyel (Van Nostrand Reinhold), the *International Dictionary of Management*, by Hano Johannsen and G. Terry Page (Kogan Page), and the *Dictionary of Business and Management*, Jerry M. Rosenberg (John Wiley & Sons).

Many notable management writers and thinkers have contributed to the ideas and definitions in the book: I should especially like to record my gratitude and debt to Peter F. Drucker, to Kenichi Ohmae of McKinsey, to Simon Majaro and to Professor Gene Gregory of Sophia University, Tokyo. Many contributions to *Management Today* have also proved invaluable, and I am most grateful to their authors.

Finally, the book would not have been born without Truman M. Talley, my publisher, nor completed without the sterling aid of Anne Leguen de Lacroix. David Fraser and Clive Allen of the Haymarket Publishing Group kindly read the galleys – but it goes without saying that the responsibility for all the words on words is mine.

INDEX

(Figures in italics refer to definitions)